Fresh Encounters with Jesus

Cheri Fuller

gotandem
An Imprint of Barbour Publishing, Inc.

Print ISBN 978-1-63058-352-1

eBook Editions:
Adobe Digital Edition (.epub) 978-1-63409-729-1
Kindle and MobiPocket Edition (.prc) 978-1-63409-730-7

The authors are represented by and this book is published in association with the literary agency of WordServe Literary Group, Ltd., www.wordserveliterary.com.

Published by goTandem, an imprint of Barbour Publishing, Inc., P.O. Box 719, Uhrichsville, Ohio 44683, www.barbourbooks.com

Our mission is to publish and distribute inspirational products offering exceptional value and biblical encouragement to the masses.

Member of the Evangelical Christian Publishers Association

Printed in the United States of America.

Dedication

Jesus,
this book is for You
and all about You.

Contents

Introduction

Seeing Jesus

Seeing Jesus is what Christianity is all about. Mark it down. We are what we see. . . . Acquiring a vision of your Maker can be like starting a whole new life.
MAX LUCADO

I lifted my face to the dazzling September sun. My husband, Holmes, and I were as excited as a couple of kids before a birthday party. We had tickets for a "Balmy Day" ride; at least that's what the brochure promised: "Maine's favorite ocean day trip—enjoy a quiet boat ride to Monhegan Island—the experience will be your vacation highlight!"

As inlanders we didn't even think to check the marine forecast. The sun was shining. It was windy, but it's windy lots of days where we live, so we didn't worry.

"Are you sure you want to go?" the ticket agent at the dock asked me. "Tomorrow's going to be a better day."

That should have given me a clue, but I forged ahead. "Today's our only chance. We have to fly back to Oklahoma tomorrow," I told her.

"It's going to be bumpy out there. I could refund your money," she added. I picked up our tickets anyway, got coffee and egg sandwiches across the street, and Holmes and I boarded the *Balmy Days II* at Pier 8 with a group of other brave but naive folks.

Before we were out of the harbor, the young woman

behind me was popping Dramamine. She offered me some. "I don't get motion sickness, but thanks!" I told her with a smile.

About halfway to the island, I began to taste that egg sandwich and wish I'd taken her up on the offer of Dramamine. "Don't worry," the first mate said over the intercom, "it'll be smoother on the way back."

After an hour we arrived at Monhegan Island. We walked for a few hours around the island, strolling through art galleries and eating our picnic lunch on the big hill with a spectacular view of the ocean. Then we boarded the boat again, hoping for a smooth ride back to Boothbay.

Only a few minutes out of the harbor, the gentle rocking intensified until I felt myself slam side to side as I gripped the rail with white knuckles. Just as I readied myself for the next wave, the boat lurched forward and I almost lost my seat. The boat pitched down and rolled side to side as it moved into the wind and waves.

Every muscle in my body tensed as the cold water blowing in the cabin door splattered my sunglasses and left my hair plastered to my head. Each looming wave, I thought, might wash us into the frigid depths.

Suddenly I heard a woman on the top deck screaming in terror. The big man groaning behind me got sick all over the deck. The woman in front of me turned a grayish green, and she lay down and held on for dear life—and she was a seasoned island resident.

The captain had to steer farther out to sea in a fruitless endeavor to find calmer waters. As waves continued to crash into the boat and come over the bow, I looked up at the life jackets, wondering if we'd have to use them. A man near me saw my glance and said, "They wouldn't help us much. The water's only forty degrees." I looked over just as the first mate's book *Shipwreck* slid into the aisle.

I realized I was gripping the bench as if *I* were the one steering the boat. Anxiety rising, I had what I could only describe as a "deep connection with God." Fear, I've found, can be a great handle to lay hold of God, and it's a powerful way to experience some intimate moments with Him.

You made this wind and the waves, and You could quiet them down just like You did for the disciples! I said silently.

I've experienced dozens of moments in my life when I wished things would calm down and problems would disappear. I kept on with this line of conversation with the Lord for a while until it was clear the waves were not getting smaller. In fact, the boat was heaving even more.

Then, since You're not quieting the waves, would You speak to me? Quiet my heart and show me what You want me to learn. I waited and listened.

"*Enjoy the ride*," God seemed to say.

Enjoy the ride? I asked. Surely I heard wrong.

But again the words came: "*Enjoy the ride.*"

My husband, I noticed, *was* enjoying the ride—even soaking wet and cold from the waves that splashed over the top deck (but he also loves jumping out of airplanes).

As I pondered those words, I looked around the lower cabin to see who else seemed to be enjoying the ride. I finally spotted an old couple, tall and ruddy faced, who looked perfectly peaceful, as if they were on a happy Sunday excursion.

I inched my way to the back of the cabin, holding on as the boat rolled through its audition for *The Perfect Storm*.

"You look like you're really enjoying this. You don't seem scared or sick. What's your secret?" I asked the elderly pair.

"Just keep your eyes on the horizon. Don't look at the waves. Look out as far as you can. Keep your eyes peeled on the horizon way out there," they said, pointing to a far-distant point.

Returning to my seat, I took their advice. I discovered something amazing. A sense of peace replaced the anxiety, and I began to experience Jesus as my Prince of Peace in a real way. It was almost as if I could see Him on the deck smiling, reveling in His creation, reigning over the whole excursion.

And as I got a fresh vision of Jesus and kept my eyes on the horizon, I felt His peace that afternoon. I didn't care that the waves didn't change. They were just as choppy, and the boat still pitched and rolled wildly.

But something in *me* changed. I experienced such a strange and wonderful calm that I went out on the deck and enjoyed the splash of the ocean water on my face. I noticed how the sun was sparkling like diamonds on the water and how gorgeous the day was. I chatted with fellow travelers. A former naval officer told me about the forty-five-foot waves that had rushed over the deck of the navy ship he was on during World War II in the Atlantic. To him, these ten-foot waves were child's play. "It's all about perspective," he told me.

I delighted in the gulls flying over us in the bright blue Maine sky and the school of dolphins jumping in the choppy waters near the boat. We eventually made it back to Pier 8, and as I look back now, the ride really was the highlight of our trip.

The Christian life is rarely a calm harbor ride. It's more like an adventurous ocean excursion where the waves can be huge, the ride bumpy and uncertain or wild and difficult. Things can seem overwhelming. Sometimes we want to get off the boat, and we long for calmer waters.

Still God says, "Look at Me, not the waves. Fix your eyes on Jesus—and don't forget to enjoy the ride!" (see Hebrews 12:2). Our tumultuous boat ride reminds me of a card I saw once with a hippo in a boat surrounded by huge waves. Inside it said:

Lord, thank You for upheaval,
For rocking my little boat.
For sending winds that seem too strong
And waves that threaten to capsize me.
Because all of this drives me into Your arms.
And anything which results in that end, Lord,
Is worth getting wet over.

Being driven into Jesus' arms, I've found, is truly worth getting wet over, and even worth going through a tumultuous storm now and then.

A Fresh Encounter with Jesus

Staying focused on God in stressful times is a vital part of our spiritual journey. World-class sports stars, such as tennis champion Venus Williams and gymnast Shannon Miller, who won the most gold medals ever and is from my hometown, have been the subject of research by scientists trying to determine why they win championships against athletes who have just as much talent and skill. What is their secret? It's not just that they practice a lot or set aside distractions to hone their skills. So do other athletes. *It is their ability to stay focused under stress.* Their focus is a tennis championship, Olympic gold medal, yellow jersey, or grand slam in golf.

The Bible tells us the supreme prize is "the heavenly prize for which God, through Christ Jesus, is calling us" (Philippians 3:14 NLT). This verse tells us what our focus is to be—something more important than winning the Tour de France or gaining a world championship: knowing Jesus and following Him as He calls us from glory to glory.

Looking for God at every turn—and freshly encountering Him—keeps us focused on our purpose in life regardless of how rocky the journey is. Seeing and encountering Jesus isn't just something we "want"—like sprinkles on a doughnut—it's something we need, vital to a life of faith.

It's so easy for our spiritual eyesight to become foggy, clouded by disappointments, or marred by difficult circumstances. Sometimes we're so focused on ourselves that we can't see anyone or anything else. We begin to think the Christian life is all about us instead of all about God. Often we're like the disciples, with our eyes fixed on the trials and tumultuous waves that threaten to sink our ship. I love what Anne Graham Lotz said about this: "When we are faced with great problems, our tendency is to focus on the hands of God—what He has not done for us and what we want Him to do for us—instead of focusing on the face of God—simply who He is. Our depression can deepen through this kind of self-preoccupation. Often, in the midst of great problems, we stop short of the real blessing God has for us, which is a fresh vision of who He is."[1]

Sometimes our view of God is colored by old attitudes and impressions of Him perceived through the filter of our childhood experiences or the intensity of our present pain, as we're going to see in the chapters ahead. And even if we've been a Christian for a long time, just as a marriage can get stale to the point that we walk past our mate day after day and hardly notice him or her, we do the same with the Lord. We lose the vision of His majesty, rich mercy, and amazing loving-kindness, and we have a hard time staying connected. We can attend church services regularly and miss seeing Jesus.

Oswald Chambers said, "Being saved and seeing Jesus are not the same thing. Many are partakers of God's grace who have never seen Jesus. When once you have seen Jesus, you can never be the same, other things do not appeal as they used to do. . . . If you have a vision of Jesus as He is, experiences can come and go, you will endure 'as seeing Him Who is invisible.' "[2]

This book is all about experiencing fresh encounters with Jesus, seeing Him more clearly and letting that vision transform your life. Most of us don't need another program to attend at church, more committee meetings, conferences, or Bible software as much as we need a fresh revelation of Christ. Because when we see Jesus and encounter Him, *we are changed*! Our hearts are renewed, and we are energized to continue on God's path.

Second Corinthians 3:18 says, "We all, with unveiled face, beholding the glory of the Lord, are being transformed into the same image from one degree of glory to another. For this comes from the Lord who is the Spirit." When we see Jesus, even a glimpse, "we are transfigured much like the Messiah, our lives gradually becoming brighter and more beautiful as God enters our lives and we become like him" (2 Corinthians 3:18 MSG). Seeing and really encountering Jesus clearly changes us—it changes the way we live, including our behavior, our relationships, and our goals.

I invite you to join me as we look at five pathways through which we can have a fresh encounter with Jesus—through moments in the Word; through service; through our trials; through mountaintop experiences and events that light a fire in us; and through whispers from God's Spirit that lead to times of repentance, hearing Him more clearly, and most of all, seeing our Savior.

These pathways make up the five sections of the book. In each section, you will read stories of biblical and contemporary people, including my own stories, that point you to Christ. Each chapter will not only include a true story but also personal application points to encourage you in freshly encountering Jesus in your own life.

As we begin, here are some ways to start the journey:

Reflect. As you consider these questions, journal or discuss your responses with someone:

- When was the last time you had a real encounter with Jesus? How did this affect you or impact your life?

- What's the biggest hindrance to your spiritual journey?
- What comes into your mind when you think about God?
- When difficulties or storms hit your life, what do you tend to focus on?

In the pages ahead, we're going to look at ways to not only see and encounter Jesus in our everyday lives but fix our eyes on Him, too.

Ask. The Bible encourages us to ask, seek, and knock (see Matthew 7:7). Tell God you want to see Him as He really is right in the midst of your mundane circumstances or the chaos and changes going on in your life. This kind of seeking the face of God, not just facts about God—looking for God Himself, not just for what He can do for us—is no small thing. God loves a relentless seeker! He promises that those who seek Him will find Him: "'If you look for me wholeheartedly, you will find me. I will be found by you,' says the LORD" (Jeremiah 29:13–14 NLT). I'm so glad you joined us on this life-changing journey!

Part One

A Fresh Encounter with Jesus through the Word

Chapter 1

The Living Word

For the word of God is alive and powerful.
HEBREWS 4:12 NLT

I sat midway down the third row in a classroom full of college freshmen rattling papers and chattering nervously as the professor strolled into Religion 101. Dr. Anderson was heralded as one of the very finest, most intellectual professors in the department, and I couldn't wait to hear him teach.

Although I'd grown up in a mainline church and answered an altar call at age twelve, I had wrestled with questions about faith and Christianity for years, and the countless sermons I'd sat through hadn't addressed the many issues I wondered about, like: *Are heaven and hell really real? Is God a good God? If He is real and He's good, how can I really know Him? Does He hear our prayers and answer them, or is it just a religious exercise we're supposed to do? Is the Bible true or just a great book of stories? Is Jesus God or just a great man we are to emulate?*

So many times with great intentions I'd started the daily Bible readings recommended by our youth pastor, especially after summer mountaintop experiences at youth camp, only to have them become dry and lifeless after a few weeks. The pursuits of high school—drill team, boyfriends, AP courses, and applying to college—reclaimed my focus.

Now I can really get into the Bible. Now I can get answers to my questions, I thought as I leaned forward in my chair. Dr. Anderson greeted us, opened his lecture notes, and outlined the semester. Then, with thrilling description and characterization, he told the stories of Adam and Eve and Noah and the flood from Genesis. We sat in rapt attention at his colorful rendition of the familiar narratives. At the end of the hour-and-a-half class, he closed his lecture notebook and looked out at me and the other impressionable college students with his piercing blue eyes.

"What's most important to remember as you take this course is that these and all the stories in the Bible are merely myths that reveal to us the meaning of our life. Although they represent truth, these symbolic stories existed in ancient religions that predate the religion of the Israelites by thousands of years. Through metaphorical language, these myths make intelligible what is beyond words. They represent spiritual experience but cannot be taken literally. Forget your preconceived ideas of what you've been told about these stories from childish Sunday school applications of the Bible. I want to shake you out of your complacency."

I don't know about the other students, but I was definitely shaken out of my complacency. I had already been disappointed in God's handling of things when my father dropped dead of a heart attack, my aunt drowned tragically, and a close friend died in an accident. Now, with every word the professor spoke that semester, another brick in my already-faltering faith came toppling down. As the weeks wore on, the more he analyzed and lectured, the more I questioned the reality and truth of the Bible and who God is—or was. Oh, I still attended church now and then when a friend wanted to go, but I silently disdained the "Bible thumpers" who attended Bible studies and Friday night missions.

Yet God, who meets us right where we are and pursues us because He loves us, even when we are still sinners, saw the yearning in my heart. He saw my pain and confusion and my longing to know Him, and began drawing me back to Him through the thing I spent the most time in—the study of literature. He also was drawing me to Himself through life's difficulties and experiences, but that's another story.

As an English major, I loved all the courses required for the degree: American literature, British poetry, Continental drama, Chaucer, Shakespeare, and others. By the second semester of graduate work in English literature, I signed up for Seventeenth-Century British Poetry, not knowing that the "metaphysical poets," as the authors were called, including John Donne, George Herbert, Henry Vaughan, and others, had a passion for Christ, and their poetry reflected their vibrant relationship with Him. Merely through reading and studying their writing, God drew me a little closer as I read verses such as the following:

My Soul, there is a country
Afar beyond the stars,
Where stands a winged sentry
All skillful in the wars:
There, above noise and danger,
Sweet Peace sits, crowned with smiles,
And One born in a manger
Commands the beauteous files.

HENRY VAUGHAN

I also began reading theologians and philosophers on my search for truth and found my way to Paul Tournier, a Swiss psychiatrist who was a committed Christian; Dietrich Bonhoeffer, a German pastor imprisoned and later martyred by the Nazis for his faith; and Edith Schaeffer, cofounder of the Christian organization L'Abri, as well as other books by L'Abri authors. Quietly I read and pondered what they had written. And I continued my graduate work as I had first one son and then another, and then moved from Texas to Tulsa, Oklahoma.

Eyes Wide Open

I sat on the brown-and-gold print couch in the

living room of our little house on Delaware Place one afternoon, not knowing what to do with myself. I usually spent the boys' naptime studying for my oral exams, but only a few weeks before, I'd lumbered across the stage, seven months pregnant, and received my diploma. There was nothing left to study. I'd done everything that was supposed to bring happiness, or so I thought. I had gotten married after college. We had two precious little boys and one child on the way. We lived in a nice brick home with a white picket fence and white shutters on a pleasant street. I had finally even been able to buy the much-longed-for yellow country print curtains for our bedroom. I had finished my degree after working on it for five years, and Holmes was doing well in the clothing business.

Everything should have been fine. But at twenty-nine, I found myself asking, like the old Peggy Lee song, "Is that all there is?" There was this empty place inside that none of the above wonderful things and people had filled. I was worried about our son's persistent asthma attacks and beset by fears. Without a single good friend in the city we'd just moved to, I was extremely lonely. We were so busy in our individual pursuits that Holmes and I had become increasingly distant, and the small, daily resentments had piled up into barriers between us that seemed like the Great Wall of China. As long as I was working toward a goal, I could keep the loneliness and fear at bay. I could stuff down the unresolved losses and pain. But a darkness seemed to be encroaching that I couldn't deny any longer.

So that afternoon as the boys slept, I combed through the bookcase looking for something worthwhile to read. Nothing looked halfway interesting.

Finally, my hand hit on a dusty Phillips translation of the New Testament my husband had used in a college class. I hadn't read a Bible in a long time, but settling myself on the couch, I began to read it in the quiet as the rain splashed on the window beside me.

I started with the book of Matthew, the first book in the New Testament, and read it page after page, chapter by chapter, day after day, just as I'd read so many books before. I finished Matthew and moved on to the book of Mark, and then Luke, not missing a chapter or verse.

Several weeks later, it was time to delve into the book of John.

"At the beginning God expressed himself," said the first verse. "That personal expression, that word, was with God, and was God, and he existed with God from the beginning. All creation took place through him, and none took place without him. In him appeared life and this life was the light of mankind. The light still shines in the darkness and the darkness has never put it out" (John 1:1–2 PHILLIPS).

As I read those words, the lights went on. It was as if scales fell from my eyes and they were opened so I could comprehend the truth.

That word. . .that is, Jesus.

He was with God from the very beginning.

He created everything! Nothing was created except through Him.

In Him, in Jesus—is life, *and His life is the light of all humanity.*

I was stunned by the truth of those words as I realized Jesus wasn't just in the past, but is *now* the Living Word, that He is alive in His Word, speaking to hearts today just as He did when He walked the earth. He is the Light who came into the world to bring us out of darkness into His marvelous Light.

Jesus is alive! I was so excited you'd have thought I was Mary and had just seen Jesus appear at the empty tomb. Mere words can't express the explosion of truth and light that went on inside. *He is not a myth as my professor suggested. He is not irrelevant as culture depicts Him. He is not a God of the past who spun the world into existence and then left mankind to fend for ourselves. He is Emmanuel, God with us.* An irrepressible joy filled my mind and heart, and the presence of Christ seemed all around me and within me. As I got a fresh vision of the Savior, it would transform everything in my life: my marriage, my thinking and perspective, my relationships, my career and mission in life.

At the same moment all this joy and awakening was happening, I had a sobering sense of conviction and thought, *If this is all true, if every word in the Bible is real and authentic and from God, how should I be living?* Thus began the process of repentance. A new desire to read God's Word and His commandments to know *how* I was to live welled up in me, and from then on, I read as if that little green New Testament contained all the treasures of life in its pages—which it did!

A few days later, I was driving down a Tulsa street with my children, the sense of God's presence still very real and alive, when a still, small voice started answering my questions, beginning with, *"Heaven and hell are real and start here—which path are you choosing? Eternal life begins now, on this earth. Who will you give your life to?"* In my response of "I'm all Yours, Lord, every part of me, my today and all my tomorrows," we began a conversation that has continued to this day.

Our problems didn't disappear just because of my spiritual renewal. In fact, our son's asthma got worse; I had an active five-year-old, a three-year-old, and a newborn to care for; and three weeks after she was born, we had moved to a new city where I didn't know anyone. But now I was aware that I did not have to handle mothering, my son's asthma, the kids' earaches or chicken pox, or life alone anymore, and it made all the difference.

And though circumstances hadn't changed, it was as if I had taken off dark glasses. The grass seemed an emerald green, the sky more vividly blue. I was filled with wonder and gratitude. Things I'd encountered hundreds of times—monarch butterflies and sunsets, a basket of green apples, and new days—now were amazing to me. I was awed by the marvelous gift of my children and husband and experienced a new love for them and for people around me.

I began especially to have a new love for the Bible. Struck by the relevancy in this Living Word, I got up early each morning to read it, page by page, chapter by chapter, and line by line. I heard God speak to me in the verses and found it true over and over that "the Word that God speaks is alive and active; it cuts more keenly than any two-edged sword: it strikes through to the place where soul and spirit meet, to the innermost intimacies of a man's being: it exposes the very thoughts and motives of a man's heart" (Hebrews 4:12 PHILLIPS).

A Fresh Encounter with Jesus

God reveals Himself in the Bible and through Christ, the eternal Word. Jesus is the face of God, the visible image of the invisible God. John 1:14 says, "And the Word became flesh, and dwelt among us, and we saw His glory, glory as of the only begotten from the Father, full of grace and truth" (NASB). From Genesis to Revelation the Lord gives countless snapshots of Himself. The Bible's stories are not just nice stories, not myths that are representations of truth, but are "true truth"[1] as Edith

Schaeffer says, so that we can know Him and come to love and worship Him and surrender our lives to Him. Here are some ways to know Him better:

Lay down false notions about God from the culture. I got some weird ideas about God from my religion professor. Like me, you may have acquired false notions about Him from movies, art, or your education. God has had a colorful yet flawed movie career, and sometimes the portrayals are blasphemous. Often He is portrayed more as a caricature than the Creator of the universe. In the 1950s movie *The Ten Commandments*, God is a booming disembodied voice. In Michelangelo's famous mural *Creation of Adam* on the ceiling of the Sistine Chapel, God is a white-bearded strongman. In the 1970s comedy *Oh, God!*, he is a wisecracking, good-natured deity with a cigar. In the 1990s film *Dogma*, God is a raucous rock star. Bette Midler's Grammy Award–winning song "From a Distance" implies that God is watching us from a long ways away but doesn't have any power or involvement in our lives. One of the more recent incarnations of God was in the movie *Bruce Almighty*, in which God is humanized as a dignified higher power who sometimes posed as a janitor. "Think it's easy being the Man Upstairs?" God asks Bruce, the television reporter who's blaming him for his problems. "Then you try running the world."

Reflect on movies, books, and songs you've gotten ideas about God from. How do these line up with stories in the Word, His interactions with people, and how the Bible portrays Him? Is His loving-kindness represented and His invitation to people to enter into a new relationship with Him through Jesus Christ demonstrated?

Read the Gospel of John with the purpose of "beholding the Lord." Just as your body needs to be nourished with good food, your spiritual life needs fuel. Through His Word, Jesus can reveal Himself to you, speak to you, guide you, and encourage you. John is a terrific book of the Bible to begin delving into because it contains some of the most basic yet profound truths about Jesus Christ. Read the book of John if you've never read the Bible or are a new believer.

And even if you've read the whole Bible before, let me encourage you to read this marvelous book of the New Testament, not so much for the purpose of getting through a certain number of chapters in the week or verses in a sitting, but to "behold the Lord" as Madame Guyon, a Christian from sixteenth-century France, described. As you read, pause instead of rushing ahead to the next verse. Sit in the Lord's presence, "beholding Him," and make use of the scripture to quiet your mind:

> The way to do this is really quite simple. First, read a passage of Scripture. Once you sense the Lord's presence, the content of what you have read is no longer important. The Scripture has

> served its purpose; it has quieted your mind; it has brought you to Him. . . . The Lord's chief desire is to reveal Himself to you and, in order for Him to do that, He gives you abundant grace. The Lord gives you the experience of enjoying His presence. He touches you, and His touch is so delightful that, more than ever, you are drawn inwardly to Him.[2]

As you do this, you will not only discover wonderful truths in His Word, but you will also discover anew Jesus Christ, the Living Word.

Chapter 2

The Psalms Prescription

Christ is full and sufficient for all his people. . . .
He is a garment of righteousness to cover and adorn them;
a Physician to heal them; a Counselor to advise them;
a Captain to defend them. . .a Husband to protect;
a Father to provide; a Foundation to support.
John Spencer[1]

"You're in charge," Bill told his thirteen-year-old son, Barrett, one cold February morning, as he gave his four children big hugs.

"No, Mom's in charge, but I'll help her," Barrett answered with a smile.

"I'm going to New York City on business, and I'll be back Sunday night. Let's pray together," he said, gathering his kids and wife, Pam, around him. "I don't want to be late for my plane."

Busy with homeschooling their four children, Pam hardly noticed she didn't get a call from Bill. Three months pregnant with their fifth child, she was relieved to feel better after weeks of nausea and exhaustion. Her husband didn't call as he usually did when he was away. *No worry, he'll be home on Sunday*, Pam thought. Then they'd have a special family dinner to surprise him since they were about to close on their house. What a celebration it was going to be! Even the youngest of their four kids helped get the food and table all ready.

Five o'clock passed. Six o'clock passed. The food got cold, and still Dad wasn't home.

This is so unlike Bill, Pam thought. Voted "Most Dependable" in high school, he'd always been the perfect Christian dad and was always on time or called to check in.

Maybe his plane was delayed. A call to the airlines showed the plane had landed right on time. However, after hours of waiting, he never showed up. When Pam contacted the New York hotel where he'd stayed, security discovered his jogging clothes left in the room. She kept calling the hotel, but he wasn't seen again and didn't return for his clothes. Pam stared at the ceiling during a long, sleepless night with worst-case scenarios going through her mind.

The next day the local police department listed Bill as a missing person. Even after a thorough search by a private investigator, no evidence or sign of foul play turned up.

Bill, Pam's husband of sixteen years, had vanished.

In the course of the next year, Pam and her children struggled with overwhelming grief. She couldn't eat and became a high-risk pregnancy patient. Her fifth child, Harrison, was born six months after her husband's disappearance. He left her penniless and in a huge amount of debt he'd never revealed, and she faced the burden of stepping into the workforce. Pam loved her role as homeschooling mom and homemaker, and losing that to return to the workforce was another blow.

But the most difficult thing they faced was the unanswered questions. *Had Bill been killed? Had some horrible thing happened to him? How will we go on without him?*

A year later, when Pam and her children saw their father again, it was not around the dinner table or leading them in prayer—but on the TV news, wearing handcuffs and surrounded by law enforcement officers. His picture was splashed across state and local newspapers. He had been apprehended in another state, posing under an alias as a widower whose wife and child had died in a car wreck. Although he faced third-degree felony charges for abandoning minor children, Pam requested the charges be dropped so their family wouldn't be dragged through the courts and media. He had no desire to be reunited with his family. He didn't want to see his children or their fifth child born in his absence. He just wanted a divorce.

As the horror of what had happened sunk in, the overwhelming sense of abandonment, betrayal, and anger hit Pam in waves. *He lied to me. I'd trusted him with my life. I can't believe this has happened. How can I go on?* Sometimes her emotions immobilized her and she lay in her bedroom, shades and curtains drawn, sobbing.

One day an acquaintance knocked on Pam's door, ignoring the Please Do Not Disturb sign.

"She is not seeing visitors," said the neighbor who answered the door.

"I have to talk to Pam," Angie said. Only a few days before Bill left, the two women had met in a bowling alley during a birthday party. Pam knew Angie's husband had left her for another woman.

"How do you seem so together?" Pam asked.

"A pastor from Fort Worth shared some things with me, and the truth set me free," she said.

Pam had no idea what truth she was talking about that day, but now Angie sat beside her on the bed. "Today my Bible study teacher thanked God that He has gone before you and behind you and has a course charted for you, as He knew you were going to bear this burden."

"God knew about this? God prepared me for this?" On the one hand, it was comforting, but on the other, it knocked the wind out of Pam. *Even if I live through this, I don't want to do this. How can You declare Yourself a loving God and yet You planned to drop this in my lap?* she silently accused.

"I know the pastor would make himself available to you if you want to talk," Angie said as she left.

Pam knew she needed someone to help her make sense of her situation, but she had no faith in psychiatrists or psychologists. One had told her she ought to be hospitalized a few months after her husband had left, but the children had just lost their father. She would not allow them to lose their mother, too. When a friend had graciously sent her a thousand dollars to see a renowned psychologist in town, he asked her the same question over and over, "What happened? What happened?" He didn't offer any real hope and kept looking at his clock as if anxious for the session to be over.

One night Pam went to the Bible study hoping to talk to this pastor she'd never met. At the close of class, she gathered up her courage and asked if he could meet with her.

When they sat down on a bench outside the building, Pam poured out everything that had happened. "I feel as though I'm dying. I can get dressed, but I don't have any hope inside of me. If what life holds is poverty and work and all this overwhelming pain, I can't see why I would want to live." Then she waited quietly for the pastor's response.

"First of all, since your husband is gone and I don't know him, he will have to answer to God. But there are two paths you can go down: you can keep viewing his sins through a microscope, analyzing them and cataloging them over and over, or you can say, 'God, although I didn't cause Bill to leave, somewhere I did some things wrong. Open my eyes to see *my sin* and *my weaknesses*, and let me deal with those and confess them and praise You that You forgive me from unrighteousness, and then help me deal with forgiving Bill.'

"You see, we fight battles before the Lord in a

different way than the world does. We have to recognize that God says He inhabits the praises of His people. If God lives and dwells in the praises of His people, you invite His presence and power into your life and circumstances today through praising Him. How's your worship?"

"*Worship?* You don't understand! I am just surviving. I'm *not* in a praise mode."

"If your circumstances have obscured your view of God, then you need to correct that. I want you to read the last seven psalms, and let that be your prayer. Think of it as a prescription to take every day. Pray the verses of those psalms aloud to God, because as you declare this is the truth, no matter what the circumstances are, you will encourage your faith," he added.

"I won't feel like it. I can barely lift my voice to sing a hymn in church."

"When you ask your kids to do chores, do you let them disobey if they don't feel like it?" he asked. "Rejoice always is a command—God is saying: You *rejoice always.* You *pray without ceasing*. It's time to recognize that the Creator of the universe who is being your Husband and Provider and Father of your children is deserving of your praise. And as you praise Him, you will receive a blessing."

This sounded like harsh instructions for a woman so brokenhearted. But the next morning, Pam gritted her teeth and said the last seven psalms aloud to God, first in a monotone, purely out of obedience, not emotion.

"I will exalt you, my God and King, and praise your name forever and ever. I will praise you every day; yes, I will praise you forever. . . . The LORD is merciful and compassionate, slow to get angry and filled with unfailing love. The LORD is good to everyone. He showers compassion on all his creation" (Psalm 145:1–2, 8–9 NLT).

Tears flowed as she continued, "The LORD helps the fallen and lifts those bent beneath their loads. . . . The LORD is close to all who call on him. . .he hears their cries for help and rescues them. The LORD protects all those who love him" (Psalm 145:14, 18–20 NLT). Reading the psalms aloud to God day after day told her more about God, and she felt Him lift her up and, against all reason, give her hope.

"Lord, my life really is impossible for me; I am totally impoverished, but I'm going to praise You, and I'm going to do the next thing," Pam prayed many days as she faced the inordinate duties of single-parenting five children and juggling jobs to make ends meet. She began to see and know God in a new way. He began to show her the majesty of His Word and reveal this truth:

"Your husband is your Maker,
Whose name is the LORD of hosts;
And your Redeemer is the Holy One of Israel,
Who is called the God of all the earth.

For the Lord *has called you,*
Like a wife forsaken and grieved in spirit,
Even like a wife of one's youth when she is rejected."

Isaiah 54:5–6 NASB

Pam didn't know what it meant that God is a husband to her and father to her fatherless children, but she asked Him to show her and to bridge the gap between her head and heart.

The answer came in small glimpses and moments. One day her twelve-year-old son was playing basketball outside. As she looked at him through the window, she saw he was crying and wiping his tears on his shirtsleeve. *He needs his dad, but he isn't here. He won't ever be here.* A sense of helplessness washed over her as she realized again there was no way she could eradicate the pain of her kids.

Pam turned to God and asked, "What do You mean, Lord, You will be a father to the fatherless?"

"I didn't say I will be. I said I am a father to your son."

God was saying, "*I am,*" not "*will be,*" not "*I was.*" Not future tense, but *at that moment* and in all the moments a father is needed. *God is my children's Father. He is my Husband.* The light dawned as she got a fresh revelation of her Savior.

Yes, she'd have to accept that truth by faith, because Bill left big shoes to fill. A generous and involved dad, he had biked with his kids instead of playing golf on

Saturday. He played with them, did hobbies with them, was generous with them in meeting their needs. How could anyone fill the gaps he'd left?

Yet as Pam accepted the truth of God's fatherhood by faith, time after time He revealed Himself in a myriad of ways. Like the orthodontist who gave thousands of dollars of orthodontic work on her children's teeth. In the joy that filled their home such that people walking into their house would say, "I love to come into your home. I want my home to be like this." Through someone anonymously paying the huge cost of her children's Christian school tuition, and through mothers and fathers helping Pam shoulder the load and nurture her children. Through Uncle Gill, her brother, who included them on vacations and filled gaps in the kids' lives by going fishing and biking and playing.

Nothing changed Pam like the power of God's truth, not the psychologist or the well-meaning words of people who tried to console her. Especially in moments that threatened to overwhelm her. A few months later, the divorce decree was delivered to her. Late that night, she felt enveloped in pain as she read the words that divorced Bill from their lives forever. The dark around her pressed in. Life had seemed to unravel, and she was tempted to dwell in the past again thinking, *What happened? How can I just dismiss sixteen years of my life? How can I possibly move on?*

She pulled her Bible toward her, and her eyes fell

on verses she'd underlined long before: "'Do not call to mind the former things, or ponder things of the past. Behold, I will do something new, now it will spring forth; will you not be aware of it? I will even make a roadway in the wilderness, rivers in the desert'" (Isaiah 43:18–19 NASB). Through these verses, Pam felt the Lord's compassion and comfort wrapping around her heart, an extraordinary sense of His love breaking through even when she was preoccupied with her pain.

For many years now God has been taking care of Pam and her children, and He has never failed. Whenever they have a need, God provides. He is her Husband. He is her children's Father. That doesn't mean life has been easy or is easy right now. And though she wouldn't have planned it, she is thankful. During trials, she has prayed many times, "Whatever You want me to learn and see of You through this lack of a job or this difficulty, show me. Thank You even for the fact that I'm a single mom and have the chance to experience You as Husband and Father. If You want me to be husbanded by You for my whole life, Lord, I'll be content. You are faithful."

A Fresh Encounter with Jesus

Whether you are a single or married woman, the Bible says that your Redeemer, Jesus, the One who delivered you from the kingdom of darkness into His kingdom of light, is your Bridegroom and you are His beloved.

When you committed your life to Christ, it was as if you were at the altar saying, "I do." There are numerous references to this truth. In Jeremiah 31:32, God said He loved His people as a husband loves his wife. He told them in Hosea 2:16 that in a coming day, His people would call Him Husband instead of Master. In the same way a husband provides security for his wife, He promised in Psalm 146 that He would lead the fatherless and husbandless to security. He is forever faithful, and whether we are forsaken by husband, father, or mother, whether we are alone or surrounded by loved ones, scripture says, "the LORD will take me in" (Psalm 27:10).

Rx Psalms. For a transforming experience in God's Word, make Psalm 144 through 150, as Pam did, your prayer to God morning and evening for thirty days and see what new revelations you gain. Don't just read the verses in these psalms. Pray them aloud to God, whether you feel like it or not, as your worship of Him. I have found this is a sure prescription for depression and anxiety, and for times when I am overwhelmed. Absorbed over time, the power of God's Word will lift your eyes from the problem to who God is. The power of the Word will change your heart and life.

Let scripture bridge the gap between head and heart. Seeing the Lord as your Husband and your children's Father may be hard to relate to, so I encourage you to look up the following verses and meditate on them. As you do, ask the Holy Spirit to bridge the gap between your head and your heart so these truths will sink in:

> *The Lord. . .cares for the orphans and widows.* (Psalm 146:9 NLT)
>
> *"Your Creator will be your husband; the Lord of Heaven's Armies is his name! He is your Redeemer, the Holy One of Israel, the God of all the earth."* (Isaiah 54:5 NLT)
>
> *As the bridegroom rejoices over the bride, so shall your God rejoice over you.* (Isaiah 62:5)
>
> *"Return home, you wayward children," says the Lord [to the children of Israel], "for I am your master."* (Jeremiah 3:14 NLT)

Chapter 3

A Vision That Endures

Once it was the blessing,
Now it is the Lord;
Once it was the feeling,
Now it is His Word.
Once his gifts I wanted,
Now the Giver own;
Once I sought for healing,
Now Himself alone.
A. B. Simpson[1]

"Come and see me when you can, darling. I am always ready to entertain my sweet Robert," said the note Hannah found in her husband's coat pocket as she was sorting his clothes on her annual closet-cleaning day. Brokenhearted, she threw the love letter from her husband's mistress into the fire and pondered what had gone so wrong in their marriage. The discovery of her husband's unfaithfulness was devastating, yet Hannah Whitall Smith didn't succumb to despair. As had happened many times when waves of tragedy or disappointment rolled over her life, she turned to Christ. That very night, she dried her tears and answered a letter from a depressed unmarried friend from England who asked how she could face the loneliness of her single life:

> In my own case, I just determined I would be satisfied with God alone. I gave up seeking after any feeling of satisfaction. I said, "Lord, Thou art enough for me, just Thyself, without any of Thy gifts or blessings. I have Thee and I am content. I will be content. I choose to be content. I am content." I said this by faith. I still have to say it by faith often. I have to do so this very evening, for I am not very well and feel what I expect thou would call "low." But it makes no difference how I feel. He is just the same, and He is with me, and I am His, and I am satisfied.[2]

This was not the first time pain had touched Hannah's life. She lost four of her children to death. Her husband suffered several breakdowns and initiated an adulterous scandal that brought national humiliation and destroyed his ministry. He left the faith, and his immoral behavior was a consistent thorn in Hannah's flesh. Her three grown children rejected Christianity and embraced the liberal philosophies of the day. One daughter abandoned her husband and children for a lover; the other married one of the boldest atheists of their time. Hannah suffered financial reversals, shunning by the Quaker family and church she'd been raised in, family problems, and difficulties. Surely all this would be enough to turn her into a depressed, defeated Christian.

But instead of these trials sinking Hannah's faith and silencing her hopeful writing and preaching, they were a gateway to closer dependence on God. She remained to the end of her life a faithful wife, mother, and grandmother. She wrote the beloved classic *The Christian's Secret of a Happy Life* and other works that have encouraged the spiritual journey of millions of believers. How could this woman endure such testings and live an abundant, overcoming life?

Hannah Whitall Smith was sustained by a vision of the steadfast love of Christ—a love awakened in a life-changing revelation many years before. Because of the experience, she knew how to find her joy in this God of all-embracing comfort no matter what happened.

Hannah was a birthright Quaker born in 1832 into a loving family in Philadelphia, Pennsylvania. Her father, John Whitall, owned a large glass plant in New Jersey, and her mother, Mary, provided an environment where lively Hannah and her three siblings grew and thrived. She had a happy childhood she described as "one fairy scene of sunshine and flowers."[3] As a teenager she wished for nothing else, and only one thing marred her joy: an aching void in her heart. She knew she wasn't prepared for eternity and didn't feel she ever would be.[4]

A tireless seeker with an adventurous spirit, Hannah wrestled with the conflict between stern demands of Quaker piety and her desire to experience, learn, and celebrate life and God. At age nineteen a new life began when she married Robert Pearsall Smith, also a birthright Quaker. After a proper courtship, they settled in Germantown, Pennsylvania.

While Hannah questioned the beliefs of her Quaker religion (she felt herself very rebellious and wanted to be "good" but never seemed to fit the Quaker mold), she wanted a closer relationship with a living God. She had a longing for joy and peace but not the faintest idea what it meant to "put one's trust in Jesus." In vain she tried to work out her soul's salvation and righteousness in her own efforts.[5]

In her teens and early twenties, Hannah felt in a hopeless spiritual state, cut off from God entirely. . .like a sinking boat.[6] She grew up believing God was selfishly "intent on His own honor and glory. . .so absorbed in thoughts of Himself and His own righteousness as to have no love or pity to spare for the poor sinners who have offended Him."[7] She wondered if God was so good how He would make people who are so bent toward evil. If He was so powerful why He didn't give people the power to live in the light instead of darkness. The picture of a stern, harsh God she'd developed in solemn Quaker meetings wasn't a God she could trust or believe in. "A thousand questions rush in on every side," she said, and concluded, "I am a skeptic!"[8]

This state of unrest and darkness of spirit persisted for over two years. Her soul hungered after God, but she wasn't able to find Him. Her Quaker teaching had led to much self-examination and self-absorption. But while she endeavored to muster up inward emotions or a righteous attitude toward God, it only made her religious life miserable.

It was the death of her first child, beloved five-year-old Nellie, that brought a turnaround in Hannah's spiritual life. After Nellie died, Hannah struggled not only with grief but with an even more profound sense of distance from God. She couldn't bear the thought that her darling child had "gone out alone into a Godless universe" and yet, no matter where she turned, there was no ray of light.[9]

One day at noon, Hannah went out to a religious meeting in one of the busiest parts of the city. As she waited for the speaker to begin, suddenly "an inner eye. . .opened in my soul, and I seemed to see that after all God was a fact—the bottom fact of all facts—and the only thing to do was to find out all about Him."[10]

From that point on, Hannah couldn't rest until she knew Him and realized that the Bible was the book she needed. When she went to the beach with her family a few weeks later, she took only her Bible and a determination to find God. Sitting in the sand under an umbrella each day, she read the book of Romans, where she discovered that "while we were yet sinners, Christ died for us" (Romans 5:8 KJV). Here she had her first glimpse of God as He is revealed in the face of Jesus Christ. Her vision of the great unselfishness of

God made her "radiantly happy,"[11] as she knew without a shadow of a doubt that all people were sinners and therefore all deserved punishment. But Christ had taken our sins upon Himself and had borne the punishment in our stead. He had forgiven us and let us go free. She didn't have to *try* to be righteous or pious. Christ had paid the price and offered her His righteousness.

"It was all outside of oneself, and there need be no searching within or rakings up of one's inward feelings to make things right with God," she said.[12] In these moments in the Word, God's extravagant love not only healed and comforted her grief, but also brought salvation to her soul. She received forgiveness for her sins; "old things passed away" and the new came as she was restored to right relationship with her Savior.[13]

Hannah knew now that God wasn't a far-off, unapproachable Being,[14] but a perfect, loving, entirely unselfish God whom she could worship and adore. All her fear of Him had vanished. He loved her, He forgave her. . .and all was right between them.

As a result of this blaze of illumination,[15] her desire from that moment on was to live a life abandoned to Christ. The truths in the New Testament became her anchor, all doubting was ended, and her joy became the gladness in knowing Christ as her Redeemer.[16]

Hannah loved nothing better than to share the truths she'd discovered from God's Word with everyone she met. With this came a terrible burden for the sins of those who were lost and would be separated from God for eternity. How could God possibly bear this? She felt such pain over the desperate, lost people she saw that when she went out on the streets of Philadelphia to events or speaking engagements, she began wearing a heavy dark veil over her face to avoid looking on the faces of sinners. She "imagined these faces lost in hellish fire forever" if they were without Christ.[17]

One day the heaviness was too much to bear and she cried out to God for "some ray of light, some illumination" on the matter.[18] That afternoon traveling across the city on a tramcar to speak, her eyes were covered by the veil. But when she looked out of the veil to give the conductor her fare, she glimpsed the worn, sad faces of the two men sitting next to her. Her heart broke for them, and again she silently cried out to God concerning how, in His mercy, He could condemn souls like these two men to eternal damnation.

The voice of the Spirit answered, *"It is not my will that any should perish but that all should come to eternal life."* For the second time in her life, a glorious light dawned. God wasn't a selfish God, visiting His love only on some of His creatures. He was love in its very essence. Love was the very law of His being. If she could love her children whether they were bad or good, then God must have something like a mother's love, too—only infinitely more vast and superior to her own. She also saw that God's love was not just available for a few of

His creatures, as was taught by most religious doctrines of her time, but that the sinners she'd met in the street and in the tramcar were also God's precious children.[19]

In the years that followed until her death, those early glimpses of Christ's love in the here and now were enough to ravish Hannah's heart and inspire books and messages that have impacted millions of people even into the twenty-first century. Her vision of Jesus helped her get a "firm grip on one magnificent foundation truth that nothing has ever been able to shake, and this was that God was in Christ reconciling the world unto Himself. . .the grand central fact of God's love and God's forgiveness,"[20] on which her soul could rest forever.

A Fresh Encounter with Jesus

Encountering Jesus is a wonderful thing. But the amazing thing about Hannah Whitall Smith was that she didn't lose her vision of the love of Christ though she endured "troubles and hardships and calamities of every kind" (2 Corinthians 6:4 NLT). Among the volumes she wrote, she shared some of the secrets that kept her vision of Christ alive and led to a happy Christian life—and they have great application for us today:

Live the life on wings. Hannah Whitall Smith believed our souls were made to "mount up with wings like eagles" and that they could never be satisfied with anything short of flying.[21] We try to look for help in outward things like a change in circumstances, a change in marital partners, or a change in our financial situation to free us from the things that frustrate us and defeat us. Yet no earthly refuge can truly give the deliverance we long for. Instead, we are to cast every care on the Lord and live the "life. . .hidden with Christ in God" (Colossians 3:3) on the wings of Surrender and Trust.[22] It is then, she taught, that we are raised into the "clear atmosphere of His presence" above our disappointments, thwartings, persecutions, worst enemies, provoking friends, and trials of every sort.[23]

Focus on the facts instead of feelings. Our spiritual lives can be revitalized when, as Hannah did, the old fruitless self-absorption is replaced by centering our lives on the glorious Good News declared in the Bible. Hannah persevered with unflinching faith because she believed God's Word, and it, rather than her feelings, was her foundation. She encourages us to not base our faith on emotion but on the nature and character of Christ and His unshakable promises. We no longer fix our thoughts on *How do I feel?* but on *What does God say in His Word?*

Realize that nothing can separate you from God's love. Without our trials and hindrances, our wings would be unused and thus wither and lose their flying power, Hannah taught. And yet no matter what happens, no prison or earthly walls can keep us from God. She believed, as Paul did, that *nothing* can separate us from the love of God. He wrote:

I am convinced that nothing can ever separate us from God's love. Neither death nor life, neither angels nor demons, neither our fears for today nor our worries about tomorrow—not even the powers of hell can separate us from God's love. No power in the sky above or in the earth below—indeed, nothing in all creation will ever be able to separate us from the love of God that is revealed in Christ Jesus our Lord.

Romans 8:38–39 NLT

Take a deep breath and receive this amazing truth: *Nothing can ever separate you from God's love for you in Christ. Nothing. Ever!* Therefore, "God is enough! God is enough for time; God is enough for eternity. GOD IS ENOUGH!"[24]

As we mount up with wings from our current trial with that kind of assurance, we can praise God in the face of any earthly shaking or problem, for as Hannah said, "The only creature that can sing is the creature that flies."[25]

Part Two

A Fresh Encounter with Jesus through Service

Chapter 4

The Bread of Life

A way of satisfying our brethrens' hunger
is to share with them whatever we have.
MOTHER TERESA

The morning light beamed in my office window as I pored over my notes for the messages for an international trip. In only a few days, my husband, Holmes, and I were leaving, and I had mounds of preparation ahead of me.

The more I labored, the more my sense of inadequacy grew. *The women coming to this retreat are missionaries, people with years of ministry experience and extensive knowledge of God and the Bible*, I thought. (You have to understand that some of my greatest heroes are missionaries like Amy Carmichael, Lottie Moon, Isobel Kuhn, and Gladys Aylward, and I am awed by their faith and courage.) *What do I have to share with them that they don't already know? I ought to be sitting at their feet as they teach!*

"Oh, Lord, help!" I cried.

My thoughts were directed back to the passage from John 6 I had just been reading:

Jesus went across the Sea of Galilee (some call it Tiberias). A huge crowd followed him, attracted by the miracles they had seen him do among the sick. When he got to the other side, he climbed a hill and sat down, surrounded by his disciples. It was nearly time for the Feast of Passover, kept annually by the Jews.

When Jesus looked out and saw that a large crowd had arrived, he said to Philip, "Where can we buy bread to feed these people?" He said this to stretch Philip's faith. He already knew what he was going to do.

Philip answered, "Two hundred silver pieces wouldn't be enough to buy bread for each person to get a piece."

One of the disciples—it was Andrew, brother to Simon Peter—said, "There's a little boy here who has five barley loaves and two fish. But that's a drop in the bucket for a crowd like this."

Jesus said, "Make the people sit down." There was a nice carpet of green grass in this place. They sat down, about five thousand of them. Then Jesus took the bread and, having given thanks, gave it to those who were seated. He did the same with the fish. All ate as much as they wanted.

When the people had eaten their fill, he said to his disciples, "Gather the leftovers so nothing is wasted." They went to work and filled twelve large baskets with leftovers from the five barley loaves.

John 6:1–13 MSG

As I read those words, God said, *"Just like the little boy did, offer the bread that you have. Give it to Me, and I will bless it and multiply it to feed all those you are to speak to in Thailand."*

So I stacked up the folders of message notes and outlines, offered them up, and earnestly prayed, "Jesus, be very present to take what I bring, and distribute and multiply it in the marvelous way only You can, throughout each message and opportunity and need we see." I continued preparing my messages but was aware that something had changed. My focus had shifted from *my inadequacy* to *Christ's ability*.

After twenty hours of flying time, we arrived at the airport in Bangkok. Then, following an hour of going through customs and the passport line, directed from place to place by people chattering in Thai, which we couldn't understand, we searched and searched for the Irish pastor who was supposed to pick us up. It was after midnight, and we were exhausted as we combed the sea of faces.

Finally, I went up to an English/American-looking couple and asked if they were our ride. They weren't, but they called the Overseas Missionary Fellowship (OMF) office and found that the man scheduled to pick us up wasn't coming, so we were to take a taxi to a hotel and come back to the airport in the morning to catch our flight for Chiang Mai.

I was irritated and tired, inwardly grumbling that

things had gone awry on our first night. It seemed my "bread" was already shrinking. But on the flight north to Chiang Mai, on the little plane after twenty-four hours of travel, I was encouraged by the verses in my morning reading: "God is able to bless you abundantly, so that in all things at all times, having all that you need, you will abound in every good work" (2 Corinthians 9:8 NIV), and "This service that you perform is not only supplying the needs of the Lord's people but is also overflowing in many expressions of thanks to God" (2 Corinthians 9:12 NIV).

We arrived in hot, humid Chiang Mai to the smiles and warm welcome of Larry and Paula Dinkins and Judy Clark, the pastor's wife, who held bouquets of beautiful flowers. It was the rainy season, and even when it wasn't raining, Holmes and I looked as if we'd been in a rain shower because we'd break out in a sweat as soon as we stepped outside in the heat.

On the way up the mountain to the retreat location, we stopped at Agape House, the AIDS/HIV orphanage, to pray for babies and young children. We saw God's grace in abundance in the bright eyes of the children and in the sacrificial giving of the volunteers.

That weekend I spoke to women from Sweden, Zimbabwe, Ireland, Australia, England, America, France, Switzerland, Germany, Burma, India, Thailand, New Zealand, and other countries—awesome missionaries from OMF, Pioneers, Vista Pacific, Wycliffe

Bible Translators, and other organizations.

At the last moments before a message, a different story would come to my mind, a little change in direction or scripture I hadn't thought of. New bread! That weekend I discovered that missionaries are just like you and me: they become broken or weary, in need of Christ's bread and His refreshment for their souls.

As the weekend was coming to a close, I awakened at 6:00 a.m. Sunday morning violently ill with an intestinal bacteria. Cramping, high fever, and severe headache flattened me. I somehow dragged myself to the last worship time and got in the car for the trip to the city, where that night I was to speak for two hours at Chiang Mai International Church's Sunday evening services.

How I got up to "preach" (as the missionaries called it, although I can assure you I'm not a preacher) for two services back to back as sick as I was is still a mystery to me, but although I felt very ill, God gave grace and strength the moment I got up from my chair, and He passed out much "bread." Then I'd get nauseated and have diarrhea all over again.

On Tuesday morning, Paula Dinkins, the missionary hosting us, drove me to speak to a group of Christian ethnic-Thai mothers. My heart was moved by seeing mothers' hearts so universally burdened for their children and so eager to hear how to pray for their sons and daughters. These Thai mothers were desperately worried about their children getting a good education and anxious about their kids' bad friends, materialism, and drugs. They soaked up every scripture and word of hope, and then we all prayed together for their children.

That evening a large group of Chinese Thai men and women gathered—professors, medical doctors, a lawyer, a publisher, and other professionals—and I spoke with the assistance of a brilliant translator, Wan, a PhD from Columbia University. These intellectual Asian people were very intense about wanting to help their children succeed and grow as Christians. The next evening, I remarked to Holmes, "Honey, I'm all finished, at least with the big gatherings," and breathed a sigh of relief.

However, right after we returned from the school, the phone rang. It was Avis, the director of Agape House, telling us that little Mac, a five-month-old baby for whom we'd prayed the weekend before, had died. She asked me to speak at his funeral.

Lord, I've never spoken at a funeral service. There are plenty of ministers here who could do a better job.

"This is a *great* ministry opportunity," Paula said, urging me to say yes. As missionaries who'd been on the field for more than twenty-one years, Paula and Larry saw everything in their path as a ministry opportunity and would not hear of my not accepting this one.

By the time I finally fell asleep that night, the words hadn't come. But in the middle of the night, I was awakened and slipped to my knees to pray in the dark as rain pelted on the roof. Suddenly the words God wanted me to share at Mac's service flowed into my mind and onto paper.

When we walked in the orphanage the next morning, a crowd of Thai, Dutch, and British people and Agape House volunteers stood solemnly around a baby crib at Agape House. On a delicate, pale blue quilt lay the body of the baby for whom we had prayed last Friday—little Mac, all dressed up in a precious embroidered white outfit and baby socks. Above his head on the crib was a basket of the most beautiful long-stemmed pink roses I had ever seen.

After we all sang "How Great Thou Art" and "God Makes Everything Beautiful in His Time," I spoke, with Avis's husband translating. Then we sang hymns as each person took a pink rose from another basket and one by one carefully put them on Mac's body. The hot, humid room was filled with the sound of weeping and children's voices, as volunteers and nannies had other babies and preschool children sitting on their laps. They, too, brought their pink roses and laid them on the baby's crib. It was only after the service, when I was told that the group of eight volunteers who had just arrived from Holland were not believers, that I understood why the Holy Spirit gave me such a clear presentation of the Gospel to share. Once again Jesus distributed bread.

Beginning to think a little more like a missionary, I wasn't quite as surprised when another "ministry opportunity" presented itself late that Thursday afternoon.

The wife of the police chief of Chiang Mai asked me to come to a luncheon at her home the next day. She had invited her Buddhist friends and wanted me to speak to them in a private presentation of her choosing. The problem was she didn't tell me in advance what topic she was choosing!

"Lord, what do You have in mind? Prepare my heart and help me to rest in You and listen to You," I prayed that night.

I was driven to a very elegant, large home the next day, a place much more lavish than any we'd seen in Thailand, to a "Going Away Luncheon" planned by Tuk, the police chief's wife (in Thailand the police chief is as important as the mayor of a city). Gathered around the table were Thai women from the American consulate and the consulate general's office.

After a sumptuous lunch, Tuk said, "Tell us how our children can become successful in school; share with us on being a good parent." Though staunchly Buddhist, the women so desired successful children that their hearts were wide open and willing to listen to a Christian from America share new ideas and concepts with them.

After I delivered the message, with hardly time to take a breath, we were driven to the Chiang Mai airport for the long trek through Bangkok to spend the night, then board a plane for Tokyo, and after twenty-four hours of travel, to arrive back in Oklahoma City.

As I leaned my head back in the airplane seat, I

thought of all the times bread had been distributed—and who was the source of it all.

Once when the Jews were talking to Jesus, they said that Moses was the one who gave their ancestors bread from heaven to eat in the wilderness and challenged Him to show them a miraculous sign. But Jesus knew the real source of the bread the Israelites had received in their sojourn out of Egypt: "I tell you the truth, Moses didn't give you bread from heaven. My Father did" (John 6:32 NLT). So it was in Thailand. The Bread of Life had shown up and fed many people.

I had seen Jesus, who said, "I am the bread of life. Whoever comes to me will never be hungry again. Whoever believes in me will never be thirsty" (John 6:35 NLT). Getting this fresh vision of Jesus as the Bread of Life changed my perspective on speaking, serving, and ministry. It wasn't a lesson just for this one trip but for a lifetime. Now whenever I am asked to speak or serve, whether that is close by home or hundreds of miles away, I know I am to give all that I am to Jesus and simply bring the bread He's given me, asking and trusting that He will take it, multiply it, and give it to meet the individual needs of each heart. And He never fails!

A Fresh Encounter with Jesus

When we serve others, share the Gospel, or offer hope and help, we get a chance to join Jesus in what He is doing—drawing people to Himself and extending His kingdom. Here are some ways to experience and see Jesus in your everyday life:

Seize ministry opportunities where you find them. Look at unexpected happenings, interruptions to your schedule, and invitations to serve. When we respond with a servant's heart and offer the Lord all we have and are, He can take our little offering and multiply it. Or as my friend Fern Nichols told me once, "We do the small obedience and God does the grand thing."

Whether it is serving the poor, speaking, teaching a group of kids, leading a women's ministry, loving your neighbor or family, or working in a job, remember who your source of life is and point people to *Him*. Give God the credit as people are blessed. It's all His plan, and He lets us partner with Him in doing our part. Jesus said, "This is what my Father wants: that anyone who sees the Son and trusts who he is and what he does and then aligns with him will enter *real* life, *eternal* life. My part is to put them on their feet alive and whole at the completion of time" (John 6:40 MSG). Ask the Lord, "What's my part?"

Striving is doing things in our own strength, worrying about pleasing people with our performance. Working while resting is doing our preparation and yielding to God, but letting Him do the work through us. And as we work resting rather than striving, we will see Jesus more and more because He will be the One doing more than we could ask or think (see Ephesians 3:20–21).

Much of the striving we do in life doesn't produce lasting results anyway. But what the Lord Jesus does through us, that bread we offer from Him to others, nourishes their "lasting life." As we simply do our part, we can trust the results to God. And as we invite Christ to use us, great things can happen. God is always doing great things whether or not we take time to notice them!

Chapter 5

The Face of Jesus

The greatest form of praise is the sound of consecrated feet seeking out the lost and helpless.
BILLY GRAHAM[1]

Richard Drake strained his eyes as he looked at the cancer cell cultures under the high-powered microscope in his laboratory at the research center. As usual, some of the experimental treatments were working and others were not. In spite of the importance of his studies, his mind kept drifting back to the congregational meeting the previous day. There was a sharp contrast between the preciseness of his work in the lab and the messiness of dealing with people and church problems.

The meeting dragged on for hours with discussion of a new construction plan, talk about the church's direction, and some serious accusations against church leadership. Because Richard was inundated with university committee work, he refused to participate in similar church committees.

However, Richard's wife, Michele, was heavily involved in church committees, and her cumulative frustrations spilled over into their normal daily routine. Differences among church members finally came to a head at the congregational meeting, prompting Richard and Michele to leave this church. Church politics was Richard's least favorite part of Christianity, and he had seen some of the worst in people he'd thought were such good Christians. In fact, there were lots of things hard to swallow about organized religion. *Where's God in all this anyway?* he wondered. *Why am I even involved with these hassles?*

Richard's mind would drift into critical questioning mode as it sometimes did at church, until the vivid memory of an experience he'd had one cold winter several years before interrupted his thoughts.

It was 1993 and Richard was researching treatments for HIV, the virus that causes AIDS. Along with many other researchers, he was trying to find a solution for the tragic epidemic. At this time, progress for treatment was slow, and new treatment strategies that later proved so effective in developed countries didn't emerge until 1996. Because all the knowledge he'd gained about HIV was from research journals and sterile laboratory experience, he began to realize he'd never seen the human side of the disease. In an endeavor to help in a more personal way, he joined a seven-member RAIN (Regional AIDS Interfaith Network) care team to provide help to local people with AIDS who'd been shunned by their families and community. Destitute and dying, they were in desperate need of help. The RAIN teams provided meals, transportation to doctor's appointments, hospital visits, and whatever was necessary to meet their needs.

This particular day, they were at John's apartment. John was the first care-partner Richard's team had contact with, and he was not an easy man to help. He was depressed and alienated from his family. Many of his friends had died from the disease. Lonely and belligerent, John's anger sometimes spewed on the team. But Richard had learned from his RAIN training not to look for any reward or blessing for himself in the ministry, so John's oppositional personality wasn't a problem. In fact, he'd grown to like John, and the team did whatever they could to help him. The RAIN network gave them a lot of training, but it didn't prepare Richard for what was going to happen.

After Christmas John became critically ill with pneumonia. For two weeks he was in and out of the hospital, but surprisingly he rallied enough to go home. However, John's health spiraled downward, and with no more insurance and a bank account drained by hospitalizations, he soon had to be moved to a friend's place.

The RAIN team volunteered to help John clean out his apartment. John lay on the couch, so weak all he could do was stare while the team cleaned, packed, and moved his furniture out. Once a tall, independent man, his body was now wasting away. Richard wished John would be like his feisty old self, but he didn't seem to have the energy to even speak.

Finally, everything in the apartment had been

moved out except the couch John was lying on. Since he didn't have the strength to walk to the car, they wrapped him up in blankets, creating a makeshift gurney. Each of the four people held a corner of the blanket, and Richard was positioned on the front right side by John's chest. Cocooned inside, his arms were folded across his chest as the team lifted him up and headed out the door to the stairs.

Little Rock, Arkansas, is very hilly, and it was a frigid day. Richard was amazed at how heavy John seemed, and the team strained and sweated as they went down the steps, trying to be as careful as possible so as not to jar him. However, as they carried John around the side of the apartment building halfway to the car, they slipped on some icy stairs and almost lost their grip on him. While trying to stabilize their hold on John, it was suddenly as if Richard was seeing everything in slow motion. Background noises faded out and everything seemed silent, still, and surreal.

As he looked down at John, both of his veiny arms had flailed out of the blanket, and with his legs still bound together like a crucifix, something incredible happened. John looked up at Richard with an expression that will be forever imbedded in his memory. Not a look of pain or fear, but of total peace and love, something Richard had never before seen on anyone's face before.

Suddenly it didn't look like John anymore. It was

another's face Richard saw. *My gosh, what in the world just happened?* he thought. Moments later the team regained control. Everything sped up to normal pace; the noises flooded in again. They walked the rest of the way down the hill with John enfolded in the blankets and loaded him safely in the back of a station wagon.

When they arrived at the friend's place, they carried John in. As they laid him down, there was a framed picture of Christ over the bed. *Not entirely a coincidence*, Richard thought. Early the next day, John was taken back to the hospital by his friend, where he died that evening.

Richard couldn't get the image out of his mind that he'd seen when he looked in John's face. It kept bugging him, and no amount of analyzing seemed to help. *Was it just the intensity and stress of moving John?* his scientist's mind wondered. *Is there a biochemical explanation for what I saw?*

At John's memorial service, he began telling his minister about what had happened. He, too, had been one of the four team members carrying John to the car and had been on the front left side of John. He interrupted Richard before he finished his description. "I know what you mean, Richard. I saw it, too. The face of Christ."

That was just what Richard had seen looking back at him from the makeshift gurney that held John's dying body—the face of Jesus. In that instant, two parts of his life—faith and science—merged into that one sacred, silent moment. He saw a glimpse of Christ in the face of that dying man, the same face of all suffering people.

Richard continued his work, but the research on HIV/AIDS began to change dramatically. New effective HIV treatment regimens were developed and given to patients earlier, which not only made a dramatic difference in their quality of life but also increased the survival rate.

Richard and the RAIN team cared for other people with AIDS. Each person was different. But Richard never forgot John and the image he'd seen while caring for him.

Like the disciple Thomas, Richard tends to question and doubt. As a scientist who endeavors to unlock the mysteries of our biological systems, critical analysis is hard to turn off when he goes to church. And whether he's questioning doctrine, frustrated with petty quarrels and power struggles on church committees, or disillusioned with a minister who has fallen into sin, it's that vision he saw that winter day that grounds him, draws him back to God, and somehow renews his faith. It reassures him that our Lord is truly alive and that He comes to us in many different ways.

Richard hadn't looked for a blessing in serving someone who was suffering. But he experienced something that had a profound personal impact. And through the years, he's drawn on the encouragement he gained from that glimpse into the unseen when the Lord made Himself evident to him.

It shouldn't surprise us that one can encounter the Lord while serving a sick or suffering person. Jesus said:

> *"When the Son of Man comes in his glory, and all the angels with him, then he will sit upon his glorious throne. All the nations will be gathered in his presence, and he will separate the people as a shepherd separates the sheep from the goats. He will place the sheep at his right hand and the goats at his left.*
>
> *"Then the King will say to those on his right, 'Come, you who are blessed by my Father, inherit the Kingdom prepared for you from the creation of the world. For I was hungry, and you fed me. I was thirsty, and you gave me a drink. I was a stranger, and you invited me into your home. I was naked, and you gave me clothing. I was sick, and you cared for me. I was in prison, and you visited me.'*
>
> *"Then these righteous ones will reply, 'Lord, when did we ever see you hungry and feed you? Or thirsty and give you something to drink? Or a stranger and show you hospitality? Or naked and give you clothing? When did we ever see you sick or in prison and visit you?'*
>
> *"And the King will say, 'I tell you the truth,*

when you did it to one of the least of these my brothers and sisters, you were doing it to me!' "

MATTHEW 25:31–40 NLT

A Fresh Encounter with Jesus

How do you and I get a new glimpse of Jesus? Mother Teresa said it is Jesus we serve in the poor, so as we get closer to them and each other, we get closer to Christ.[2] Richard and his team only reached out to one man to start with, and their efforts may seem like a drop in the bucket with the worldwide problem of AIDS. Mother Teresa felt the same way. "I picked up one person," she said. "Maybe if I didn't pick up that one person I wouldn't have picked up the others. The whole work is only a drop in the ocean. But if we don't put the drop in, the ocean would be one drop less. Same thing for you. . . . Just begin. . .one by one."[3]

Here are some ways we can begin, one by one, to get a fresh vision of Jesus through serving others and especially the "least of these":

Take care of those at home and ask God to expand your heart. "Love begins by taking care of the closest ones—the ones at home. Let us ask ourselves if we are aware that maybe our husband, our wife, our children, or our parents live isolated from others, do not feel loved enough, even though they may live with us."[4] But as you love those close to you, don't neglect to look around to those who are sick, those battling with addictions, those who are poor or lonely whom you could care for, befriend, or join with others to minister to. Ask the Lord to expand your heart beyond the borders of your own family and fill it with His love for the broken and needy. It is in doing the work of Jesus and allowing Him to love others through us that we experience Him in new ways.

Ask God to make you willing: "Lord, let me be Your hands and feet. Show me what's on Your heart for those around me, and give me a servant's heart, a surrendered heart, and eyes to see people the way You see them."

Be open to different ways the Lord Jesus may reveal Himself to you. In J. B. Phillips's classic *Your God Is Too Small*, he said, "We can never have too big a conception of God, and the more scientific knowledge. . .advances, the greater becomes our idea of His vast and complicated wisdom."[5] Our spiritual lives are hindered by putting God in a box and only expecting to experience Him in church or in an activity designed to nurture our own souls. We may expect to sense His presence when we are listening to an inspiring worship CD, participating in a special conference, or worshipping at an extravagant Christian concert.

But my friend Kay sees Jesus in the faces of children in the hospital playroom who are battling cancer. As she helps these kids create art projects to take their minds off painful treatments, she encounters God in amazing and unforgettable ways. My friend Tony, who volunteers at a daily breakfast for homeless people, encounters Jesus again and again as he serves pancakes and sausage and gives food baskets away. Mary Ann sees glimpses of the love of Christ in foster mothers she works with in Child S.H.A.R.E., a ministry to provide homes for neglected children.

What unexpected places might you see Jesus in your world? What are the things you see in your community or world that break your heart or you can't stop thinking about? Perhaps it could be while working with children. Jesus put a little child in His arms and said, "Anyone who welcomes a little child like this on my behalf welcomes me" (Mark 9:37 NLT). It could be on a mission trip or in a nursing home. Whatever it is, this may be a key to where God is leading you to serve others and in the process see anew the King of kings, who took up His towel to serve His disciples and poured out His life that we—and the whole world—might not perish but have eternal life.

Chapter 6

An Expectant Heart

Those who keep speaking about the sun while walking under a cloudy sky are messengers of hope, the true saints of our day.
HENRI J. NOUWEN[1]

Simeon willed his aged legs to carry him quickly to the temple courts. A sense of urgency consumed him. He nodded to those who stopped to call out his name in respect, but he didn't stop to pass the time of day. He wasn't sure why or what lay ahead, but today was an important day. He recognized the powerful but tender nudging of the Holy Spirit (see Luke 2:27). It was vital that he be present in the temple courts, and he hastened to obey that calling.

When Simeon arrived, he bent to catch his breath. Once his heart slowed down, he stood and gazed at the temple. It was in this place that he felt the most at home. He had spent his life studying the Law and serving God. He loved to share the stories of the Lord's great deeds and the rich history of the Jewish faith with the younger ones who clamored to hear him. He was a prophet, a man of God, and the temple was his sanctuary—not a mere building, but a consecrated place. This was where he could give back to God what he had been given so generously. This is where he worshipped day after day. Many listened when he spoke, but Simeon did not seek man's approval. His only desire was to please and serve God.

As Simeon climbed the steps, the catch in his chest deepened. He knew that he was in the end stages of his life. He was far along in years and his body was weary. All that remained before he went on to his eternal reward was the fulfillment of a promise. Years ago it had been revealed to him by the Holy Spirit that he would not die until he had seen the Messiah (see Luke 2:26).

A breeze pushed his robes against his ankles as his thoughts scattered from curiosity to expectation. Perhaps it would be a day like today when he saw the King of kings. Would He wear a crown? Would He be a warrior with courage to lead His people to victory?

His thoughts were interrupted when the gate opened and a couple entered the courtyard. The man was dressed like a laborer, a craftsman. He clutched a crude cage in his hands, which contained two pigeons pushing against one another as he walked. His young wife walked closely by his side, a tiny baby snuggled in her arms. Simeon nodded. Today must be the fortieth day after the birth of the child. According to the Law, two pigeons or two doves would suffice for the purification offering when a family could not afford a lamb.

As the mother glanced his way and their eyes met, something in Simeon's soul quickened. He held out his arms, and the mother tenderly handed him the babe. Simeon gazed at the child. Suddenly years of intellectual knowledge were replaced by a sense of awe as he looked into the infant's face. He wasn't sure how he knew, but every fiber of his being confirmed what his heart told him. He had studied about Him, spoken to others about His coming, encouraged fellow Jews to put their hope in Him. But now as he looked into the eyes of the child, the truth burst through his soul.

This was the Messiah!

A tiny babe! How could it be? "Where was He born?" he asked.

"Bethlehem," the father replied solemnly.

"Bethlehem!" Just as Isaiah had prophesied! Simeon lifted the baby in the air, and praise erupted from the depths of his soul. The joy was like an overflowing spring of sweet water as he sang, "Sovereign Lord, as you have promised, you may now dismiss your servant in peace. For my eyes have seen your salvation, which you have prepared in the sight of all nations: a light for revelation to the Gentiles, and the glory of your people Israel" (Luke 2:29–32 NIV). Simeon rejoiced before God as if he were a man reborn.

He nestled the child against his chest and stood before the young couple. The mother's eyes were damp as she smiled through her tears. The father's face shone with humility at the words spoken by the prophet (see Luke 2:33). Simeon reached out and blessed the young family, his heart full of happiness yet heavy as the reality of the scriptures imprinted in his mind became clear.

"Young mother," he said, placing the child back in her arms. "This child is destined to cause the falling and rising of many in Israel." He shared the hard truth of the future of the Promised One. "A sword will pierce your own soul too," he said sadly (Luke 2:34–35 NIV). The couple solemnly nodded as if the words revealed what they already knew in their hearts.

Not far away, the sounds of a woman worshipping God filled the air. She had risen from her knees to stand and watch Simeon as he rejoiced with the child in his arms, but her praises continued to flow. "It is Anna," Simeon told the couple. "She is a prophetess, a righteous woman."

Anna's husband had died young, and she had been a widow for eighty-four years. She could have withdrawn from God in her grief when "death ravaged her home, but she did not bury her hope in a grave. . . . In place of what God took, He gave her more of Himself. She became devoted to Him who had promised to be as a Husband to the widow and in her long widowhood was unwearying in her worship."[2]

Anna had devoted her life to praying for others, crying out day and night to God. She was thin, for she fasted continually.[3] The sight of Anna kneeling in worship and prayer in the temple court was as familiar a sight as the sun that shone each morning.

She hesitated for a moment then walked toward

Simeon. "Could it be?" she asked. Her weathered face gazed at the child, hope in her eyes. Like Simeon's, Anna's mind was saturated with Old Testament prophecies and promises concerning the coming of the "seed of the woman to bruise the serpent's head."[4]

Simeon nodded. "Yes, Anna, it has come to pass," he said. "The Messiah is here!"

After gazing upon the face of the Christ child, basking in the goodness of God to send His Son for a few precious moments, she turned and ran. Her back was bent with age, but her steps were quick as she spilled the news to those who had gathered around the courtyard.

"The redemption of Israel has arrived!" she called out (see Luke 2:38 NIV). "The Messiah has come!" Though her eyes were failing from age, they shone brightly from those few moments of seeing Jesus, and tears of joy slipped down her cheeks.

These two godly servants, Simeon and Anna, played no great role on the stage of Bible history. Some might even call them "bit" players, yet God chose them to be witnesses. They were chosen to confirm what had been spoken generations before. It was no accident that they were in the right place at the right time. They were expecting God, and when He called, they heard His voice.

Simeon's and Anna's hearts were fixed on something they could not see. Their attitude was that of worship as they waited on God's timing. Until the moment that Simeon saw the baby Jesus, he lived by faith alone. The joy he expressed as he sang praises in the temple court was that of a man who had seen a promise fulfilled right before his eyes. Until he saw Jesus, his mind was brimming with knowledge about the Chosen One, but to see Jesus in the flesh was the fulfillment of all he had believed and hoped for. Simeon was so satisfied with the vision of Jesus that he experienced total peace. One glance had given him all he needed to move on to his heavenly reward.

Anna, too, had lived a life of faithful service and devotion. As one widowed in her youth, she was left "desolate" and perhaps had faced a "long, lonely, and cheerless" existence.[5] Yet she gave her all to God, going to the temple faithfully, each mundane day after day and year after year to pray for the coming of the Messiah. When the miracle occurred and He was brought to the temple by His mother and father, her faith, like Simeon's, was rewarded.

A Fresh Encounter with Jesus

Have you ever served God faithfully while waiting for His promises to come to pass, yet all you see are delays? Have you experienced the hope that when deferred makes the heart sick? (See Proverbs 13:12.) Sometimes it's hard to hold fast when daily circumstances contradict God's promises. Simeon and Anna were able to wait with hope because they fixed their eyes on God alone. Since they were both elderly and the promise was a long time in coming, they could have become disappointed in God and dismissed the nudge of the Holy Spirit when the young couple arrived in the temple court.

The king Simeon and Anna expected was a warrior, not a baby in the arms of a young woman. By appearances the couple that came into the temple that day was poor. But because Simeon and Anna lived a life of expectancy, they recognized the unlikely answers that only God could have delivered. We, too, can receive the promise if we do the following:

Live expectantly, tuned in to the Spirit. When we seek God, we learn to recognize the voice of the Holy Spirit. We become sensitive to that prompting and are available when God calls us to witness His handiwork. We can find comfort when we are tired or impatient to see those promises take place. The Holy Spirit can show us things that others might not see or understand, just like when He promised Simeon that he would see the Messiah before he died. But we are unlikely to hear that voice unless we prepare ourselves to do so by seeking God. The Lord becomes real and our hearts become expectant as God provides a fresh vision of Himself in our quiet times with Him. Just as He did for Simeon and Anna, God will kindle the joy in your soul when the knowledge about Him is transformed into relationship with Him. It can be like seeing Him for the very first time.

When we eagerly look for God, we may find Him in unexpected moments and even in places we've been hundreds of times. The Bible shares many promises that center around our daily lives, but we can also look forward to the eternal promise He gave each of us. *He is coming again*. That's a great hope. Just as the Holy Spirit promised Simeon that the Messiah would surely come, we have been promised that our Savior will return again for those who are looking for Him.

Let us be among those who say, "Behold, this is our God; we have waited for Him, and He will save us. This is the LORD; we have waited for Him; we will be glad and rejoice in His salvation" (Isaiah 25:9 NKJV).

Expectancy. It's an attitude of the heart.

Be a missionary. Anna not only expected good things from God, but when the promise came to pass, she shared that hope with others around her. Bursting with joy, she didn't keep the marvelous news to herself. In fact, Anna became "the first female herald of the Incarnation to all who looked for the Redeemer in Jerusalem," a true missionary.[6] We, too, have the opportunity to share the promise with those around us. And though some are called to other nations, you don't have to leave the country to share God's good news.

If you have encountered Christ, talk about His

salvation and glory with others you meet as Anna and Simeon did. When you get up each day, say, "Lord, put those in my path who are looking for You, who want to know You—prodigals who have strayed away, lost sheep who need You. Help me to see my company as a mission field, my school as a place full of people with a God-shaped vacuum inside. Give me Your gentle words to share the hope that is within me!" As we intercede for others and speak of the reality of Christ, perhaps we will be the witnesses when one of our loved ones or friends has the opportunity to look into the face of the Savior and see Him for the very first time.

Part Three

A Fresh Encounter with Jesus through Trials

Chapter 7

Climbing into God's Lap

If once we accept it as true that the whole Power behind this astonishing universe is that kind of character that Christ could only describe as "Father," the whole of life is transfigured.

J. B. PHILLIPS[1]

The last rays of the sun were going down as I sat in the living room of a friend's house with seven other women. We had prayed for the youth of our city, for our own teens and college kids, for the rocky marriage of one of the women, and for other issues. Everybody else was feeling lighthearted now, but I was still burdened about finances, work deadlines, and a struggle our daughter was experiencing.

Sitting next to me, Susan sensed my heaviness and said, "Just climb into God's lap. Let Him put His arms around you and hold you."

What an odd thing, I thought. *Climb into God's lap?* No matter how hard I tried, I simply could not relate to that picture of God or visualize myself doing this. It sounded wonderful, but I had no grid for the kind of God you could snuggle up to. I could relate to an Almighty whom I could endeavor to please or serve. But climb up into His lap and just *be*? Allow myself to rest in His arms when I was having a really bad day?

When the group broke up moments later, we fled to our minivans and the evening's activities, but those strange words kept going through my mind: *Climb into God's lap*. As the months wore on, my dilemma continued. I could relate to a God I could be obedient to and please—but cuddle up on His lap?

When I'd read my Bible daily and was "prayed up" and happy-hearted enough to encourage others around me, it was easier to approach God. But when I felt negative or sad, it was harder to receive His comforting love. And if something bad or terribly stressful had happened, I felt God had abandoned me.

What I gradually realized was that how I saw God was connected to how I related to my father and step-father. Papa showed his love by providing for and protecting us. He had a brilliant mind, and I admired and loved him—he was our hero! In fact, he was known in the family as the "Great White Father." Papa was tall, dark, and handsome, a lawyer by trade, and one of the top ten bridge players in the nation who competed internationally as part of the American team. Reserved not demonstrative. Quiet not expressive. The strong, silent type who didn't express affirmation or praise very readily.

I tried very hard to please Papa and be noticed by him, acting as "good" as I possibly could. But it was hard to gain his attention being in the middle of six children, flanked by three outstanding, beautiful older sisters (called "the big girls"), my darling, everybody's-favorite little sister, and Papa's much-awaited only son and namesake, George F. Heath Jr.

He had very high standards for his children in achievement ("You should make all As; you're all smart because you're Heaths"), but he wasn't a daddy you could run to and jump on his lap and feel his arms around you. Or maybe since we were a big group of six children closely stair-stepped in age, he would have found it difficult to get his arms around us.

Papa expected obedience, and since I'd seen his anger when he was crossed, I wanted to avoid his temper at all costs. And when he died in the middle of the night of a massive heart attack, I was left with a profound sense of abandonment a daughter experiences when she loses her father at an early age, whether by death or divorce.

With my mother's remarriage less than two years later to my stepfather, the filter I saw God through got even blurrier. My stepfather was more my mom's husband than my father, and one of his first memorable acts was taking the little terrier my dad had given Marilyn, my little sister, and me to a deserted country road and dumping him while we were at school. We never saw our beloved "Mr. Pup" again.

In realizing how my father-filters had marred my picture of God (sort of like seeing Him through dark glasses), I began taking a hard look at father issues in my life. I began the process of releasing my faulty views of God and asking Him to reveal Himself anew to me. I also found support in a small group for a time and some sessions with an insightful counselor. Over time I began to lay down the misrepresentations of God, forgive my father and stepfather, and focus on what God said about Himself all through His Word.

As I sought God in just these simple ways, by faith, not because I had a lot of feelings, what I knew about Him in my head moved to my heart. I began to sense the loving arms of my heavenly Father that had been there all the time, waiting to welcome me to His arms in the best of times and the worst of times. I felt His acceptance of me just as I was, whether that was tired or in turmoil. I didn't have to work for Him or try harder to please Him. I didn't have to achieve or wipe my tears and put on a happy face for God. I could simply *be* and experience Him as my comfort and refuge. And what amazing good news that God wasn't going to abandon me in the middle of the night or when things got difficult but promised never to leave me or forsake me (see Hebrews 13:5).

As I saw anew the One who had created me and loved me, I found a new release in prayer and a deeper sense of His presence. I realized that He didn't love me less when I was broken or sad. In fact, the Bible says He is close to the brokenhearted (see Psalm 34:18) and very near to those who are crushed in spirit. And He is the Father who comforts us in all our troubles (see 2 Corinthians 1:3–4). I discovered His open arms were ready to console and embrace when we are battered by life or circumstances, for God has said, "I will comfort you there. . .as a mother comforts her child" (Isaiah 66:13 NLT).

Because we live in a fallen world, no matter how good our earthly fathers are, they are imperfect and often misrepresent God. God wasn't like my father or stepfather, and He isn't exactly like your dad, either. He is the perfect Father (see Matthew 5:48). His love isn't available to us only when we measure up to rigid, hard-to-reach demands. And we don't have to perform to earn His love.

God is the complete expression of love (see 1 John 4:16) who is infinitely patient and eternally faithful. We already have the Lord's attention; we don't have to jump through hoops to gain it! He chose you when He planned creation (see Ephesians 1:11), and it is His desire to lavish love on you simply because you're His child and He's your Father (see 1 John 3:1).

Martin Luther, father of the Reformation, understood this concept of a God who comforts us as a child on the lap of her mother and described prayer as the "climbing up of the heart into the heart of God." But many of us don't experience God as truly the "God of all comfort" (2 Corinthians 1:3) because of the father flaws in our lives.

What can we do about these marred filters through which we see God? The first thing is to understand them and then to resolve them. Jack Frost, author of *Experiencing the Father's Embrace*, says that until the father issues are resolved through "an experiential revelation of the heavenly Father's love," a person may be a Christian for many years but find it difficult to experience the affectionate love God has for us. He describes dads in six categories:[2]

The passive father may be at home, but he isn't really "home" in terms of being emotionally available and openhearted. He is uncomfortable expressing emotion and has few hugs, kisses, and words of love. While he doesn't actually reject his kids, he doesn't embrace them, either. If you had a passive dad, your relationship with God may be characterized by discipline and duty rather than joy and a sense of being loved.

The performance-oriented dad expresses love for his children, but that love is usually tied to measuring up to hard-to-reach expectations and demands for perfect obedience and success. Frequent criticism that isn't tempered with love and praise leaves kids feeling depressed, feeling like failures, and relating to God in a performance-oriented way.

The absentee father is the dad who is not physically in the home because of death, divorce, incarceration, or abandonment (this includes 50 percent of all kids in America). Children with an absentee dad may have the double whammy of a stepfather who doesn't meet their emotional needs or is undependable. In their relationship with God, even as adult Christians, they fear that God may not be there for them.

Authoritarian fathers care more about law than love; they require their children to follow every rule and may use fear, guilt, or intimidation to control them. If you were raised by an authoritarian dad, you may see God as a sheriff or master who is more to be feared and obeyed than enjoyed.

The good father. When we have good dads who protect and provide everything we need, we tend to depend on our earthly father rather than God. And if our expectations of our "good dad" are too high, we may become disappointed when he fails to fulfill a promise he's made to us at a certain point in life.

The abusive father. Any kind of abuse—verbal, emotional, physical, or sexual—creates a deep wound in the heart of the child. Besides struggling with guilt, shame, and low self-worth, women who have been abused are left feeling fearful and distrustful of God, male ministers, and men in general. Under all those damaging emotions is a seething anger at God.

You may be thinking by now that dads just can't win. In a way that's right; we live in an imperfect world, and no father can ever meet every need and be the perfect father. Only God can fill that bill! But the good news is that the very holes in our lives that result from imperfect fathering or life's losses can be used to draw us into the arms of God.

A Fresh Encounter with Jesus

How do you perceive God? As a stern, unbending judge or policeman? As someone who, like your father, is looking to criticize your faults, or who might abandon you unless you straighten up and fly right? Does the word *father* bring up negative or positive feelings in you? We will never escape a sense of futility and frustration until we begin to see what God is really like and what His purposes are.[3] Here are some ways to begin:

Draw a "God and me" picture. To get more clarity on your relationship, draw a picture that reflects how you feel about God and relate to Him and how He feels about you. Be honest as you visually portray your relationship with God. Then share your picture with a friend or spiritual mentor. Ask that person to draw her or his own "God and me" picture and share it with you. You can learn a tremendous amount about how to pray for a friend when you understand where she or he is coming from.

Bring your faulty view of God to the cross.[4] What kind of filter colors your vision of God? Review the categories of fathers in the paragraphs above. Then put that view next to how the Bible depicts Him. (Good places to start are Psalms 23, 103, 139, 145, and 146). If your perspective of God doesn't line up with the truth of scripture, bring it to the cross. Ask for His Spirit to clean off your filter so you can see the steadfast love of the infinite God who wants to be intimate with you. Pray, "Lord, I want to know You as You really are. I want to come home to Your heart and to an intimate, trusting, loving relationship with You. Cleanse my filter. Heal the wounds in my heart from the 'father flaws' I've experienced. In every situation I go through, may my vision of You and Your flawless character grow and grow, and may I be changed in the process."

No matter how adequate or inadequate your earthly fathers were, you don't have to stay stuck in the perception of God you've carried around since childhood. You can be set free by the power of the cross. You can get to know your heavenly Father through His Son, Jesus, who gave His life for you and who is the exact representation of the Father (see Hebrews 1:3). And you can enjoy Him forever!

Chapter 8

The Lord Who Sees Me

God sees you as much as if there were
nobody else in the world for Him to look at.
CHARLES SPURGEON[1]

The thirteen-year-old waved good-bye to her parents as she stood on the porch of her grandma's house in Canada, far from where she had been raised in Brazil. Tears fell down her cheeks and a knot formed in her stomach, one so tight that it didn't go away for many years.

Terri was an "MK," or missionary kid, who grew up with her six other siblings in a lush green lumber and cattle state of southern Brazil where her parents served for most of their lives. As a young teen, she and her sister and brother were left in Canada with an elderly grandmother while her parents went back to Brazil—back to the work and ministry that was always their first priority.

Throughout her childhood, Terri lacked the security of feeling unconditionally loved and accepted. She felt little warmth or affection, as her parents held their children to high standards of performance. Discipline for minor infractions felt harsh and severe, and sadly, there were few signs of forgiveness or assurance. So

Terri and her siblings grew to know God as severe, demanding, and distant—to be feared but not embraced. To be obeyed but never enjoyed. They were all expected to grow up and be missionaries, and Terri aimed to please. She attended church faithfully and even worked for a mission organization after her marriage. She was content being a "good" Christian.

Until tragedy struck.

"I don't know what I'd do if anything ever happened to my husband," Terri had casually commented to a friend one August afternoon. "He helps me so much, I'm spoiled."

She scurried home that day just in time to kiss Bob good-bye before he left for his night job. But at four o'clock in the morning, something woke her up. She reached for her husband. He wasn't there. Suddenly she was wide awake, her heart racing. He was due home at three.

The next several hours blurred into a haze of questions coupled with the stubborn self-assurance that God wouldn't let anything happen to Bob. After all, they'd served Him in a missionary organization. Then after seven years, they'd had a sense God was stirring them to reevaluate their place of service. In the meantime, Bob was working the night shift as an electronics technician in a computer manufacturing company and planned further schooling in September. To save money, he rode a motorcycle to work.

As night became dawn and broke into full daylight, fear slowly knotted Terri's whole being.

Six o'clock. Seven o'clock. *Where is he?*

"Oh, Lord, I'm desperate," she cried. "Please let me know where Bobby is."

Turning on the radio for comfort, she listened to a traffic report. Then she heard it. "An injured motorcyclist is being treated at USC Medical Center."

Questions without answers tumbled over each other in her spinning head. Shaking, she dialed the hospital.

"Yes, there's a Bob Geary here," the receptionist drawled. "But I can't tell you anything. You're gonna have to call later."

While struggling to hold back her tears, she dressed, fed her children, and arranged for their care so she could go to the hospital.

"Mrs. Geary," the doctor said brusquely in the ER waiting area, "your husband's spinal cord is severely injured. He is paralyzed from the shoulders down. And if he lives, he'll never walk again."

If he lives? Paralyzed? Never walk? Disbelief, confusion, shock, and anger flooded over her. *He's wrong! God wouldn't let this happen!*

Terri was directed to the ICU waiting room to wait until she was allowed to see Bob. Friends stood silently by, and she was encouraged by their fervent prayers.

In the hours that followed, the story was pieced together from newspapers, TV reports, and Bob's limited input: he left work at 2:00 a.m. Halfway home on the freeway, he looked up just in time to see an eighteen-wheeler truck falling off an overpass. To avoid being crushed to death, he bailed off his bike. As his motorcycle disappeared under the truck, Bob hit the pavement, breaking his neck in the process.

It was several days later before Terri realized that if her husband recovered, he would be a quadriplegic. She hadn't the slightest idea what that meant for their life and family. In her numbness she couldn't know how deep would become the anger, depression, self-pity, and sorrow.

Life had been splintered forever.

As they left the hospital many months later, Terri and Bob joined the lonely world of the disabled. A world loaded with frustrations, discrimination, and stigma foreign to them. The daily invasion of nurses who cared for Bob's personal needs and infections, the constant waiting on him and their three children, assuming two parents' roles, and the extreme fatigue all became sources of despair. And she passionately dreaded the future.

Struggling with the challenges of life with a quadriplegic husband, Terri would just as soon not get up in the morning. She yearned for trouble-free days and longed to fly away and be at rest.

One day she read the story of Hagar in Genesis 16. Pregnant with Abraham's firstborn son, she was mistreated by Sarai, so she ran away. Hagar ran as far as she could, but an angel sent by God caught up with her near a spring in the desert, beside the road to Shur. When the angel inquired where Hagar had come from and where she was going, she answered, "I am fleeing from my mistress Sarai" (verse 8).

Terri thought, *That's what I want to do—run away—far from the constant caretaking, the financial struggles, the ever-present weariness and burdens I face 24-7*. She felt abandoned by a distant, hard-to-reach God and often was angry with Him. Her head knew all the right things about God, but her heart felt like He was a million miles away. Like a yo-yo that couldn't find a resting place, one day she felt like they'd make it; the next day she was down in the depths with her head spinning out of control—angry at herself, Bob, and most of all, God.

All it took to trigger resentment was for the attendant to fail to show up or some other key need not to be met. *Why us? Why so many extra problems? Why this stupid wheelchair anyway?* she inwardly grumbled. Sometimes she hated that wheelchair and all it represented. And like Hagar, she just wanted to find a place to hide and rest.

As Terri pondered the story, she was struck by what the angel told Hagar—go back to her mistress and submit to her. The angel left her with a promise that God would increase her descendants until they would be too numerous to count. "You are a God of seeing," and "Truly here I have seen him who looks after me," Hagar said (verse 13).

In that moment, Terri realized that God saw her, too, just as He did Hagar in the desert. She wasn't a second-class citizen or one who was forgotten by God. He remembered her and would revive her and look after her.

Seeing Jesus as One to run *to* instead of *away from*—as her refuge in her daily battles instead of an adversary trying to punish her—Terri's heart began to be transformed.

Instead of staying bitter and living in a survivor mode, she began a journey of getting to know God in the midst of the challenges. She realized she had a choice to make. She could treat God as a harsh villain, angrily gritting her teeth while stumbling through her day alone, or she could lean on the One who longed to comfort her, help her, and give her peace. It wasn't an overnight fix. The process of learning to lean on the "God of all grace" came excruciatingly slow. As difficult as Terri found yielding to be, with each cry of surrender her aching heart would declare, *Okay, Lord Jesus, I accept Your will for me today. I'm weak. . .I'm grasping hold of Your strength.*

When Terri offered herself to God in this way, He drew near with His strength. Through encouraging calls and lunch with gentle friends who listened without judging, notes in the mail, timely radio programs, or simply time to be alone with Him, God revealed His presence and love.

Although there are times when Terri needs to resurrender herself to God, she has found that the secret to experiencing His strength comes in trusting Him daily in the struggles that emerge. One day at a time.

No longer was God distant and hard to reach. He hadn't abandoned her or left her in another country while He got on with *His* ministry. And He did see right where she was. Terri finally began to experience the reality of Psalm 73:28: "But for me it is good to be near God; I have made the Lord God my refuge, that I may tell of all your works."

God graciously brought Bob far beyond medical expectations. Eventually he learned to feed himself and to drive his own electric wheelchair as well as a customized van. He dedicated countless hours of technical advice to missions organizations and became a self-made "computer guru," offering his expertise to many who couldn't afford to take their computers to be repaired. He is now battling acute leukemia.

"Yet even with the trials, looking back I wouldn't want to return to just sailing along and being a good Christian but not really knowing God," says Terri twenty years down the road. Over and over the struggles she and her husband have experienced have become a doorway to gain a fresh vision of Jesus, to see that

He is her strength when she's weak, her provider when the family has need, her rest when she's weary. She knows her Lord in an intimate way *because of* the trials and difficulties. And she knows that He who sees her loves her with an everlasting love.

Maybe, like Terri did, you feel that God has ignored you or is too busy to care about the pain in your life. The truth is, "God sees you as much as if there were nobody else in the world for Him to look at," said Charles Spurgeon. "If I have as many people as there are here to look at, of course my attention must be divided. But the infinite mind of God is able to grasp a million objects at once and yet to focus as much on one as if there were nothing else but that one. . . . God sees you with all His eyes, with the whole of His sight—you—*you*—You—YOU! are the particular object of His attention at this very moment."[2]

Whether we feel like it or not, we are an open book to God, and He knows our every thought (sometimes that can be scary!). He counts the number of hairs on our head. And there is no place we can go to avoid His Spirit or be out of His sight. If we climb to the sky, He's there. If we go underground, He's there. If we could fly on morning's wings to the farthest horizon, He is already there waiting! We are never out of His sight (see Psalm 139 MSG).

If God can see you, He can hear you. He hears your prayers, and even if you can't get a word out, He understands your tears and sighs. If it's in the middle of the night and no one is around to care for you, God is there with you. He's not slumbering or sleeping even if the rest of the world is (see Psalm 121:4). What good news—we are not alone. We are not forgotten. We are known and loved by the Lord! Here are some ways to get a fresh glimpse of this aspect of God:

Reflect on times when you feel invisible, discounted, forgotten. What triggers in you a sense that God has left you or is too busy with His work in the universe to care about your problems? For Terri, it was a tragedy that altered her life and her family. For another person, it might be a divorce, a loss of someone she loves, a financial reversal, or a job layoff. Bring these past or present experiences to God and tell Him you want to regain your spiritual eyesight and a sense of His presence. Then meditate on the whole of Psalm 139; Matthew 10:29–30; and Acts 17:28.

No matter how difficult the trial you may go through, you can expect that the Lord will ever guide you with His eye, will support you by His guardian hand, and will keep you from all evil. "The God of all grace, who called you to his eternal glory in Christ, after you have suffered a little while, will himself restore you and make you strong, firm and steadfast" (1 Peter 5:10 NIV).

Seek the face of God in the midst of trouble. When was the last time you looked for Jesus in the midst of a pressing problem? Often we say, "Lord, fix this. Change this problem. Do something about this mess I'm in!" That's okay, yet there's a real difference in praying the life-transforming prayer, "Lord, I don't understand this situation and I seem powerless to change it. But I want to see You and encounter You. Would You teach me what You want me to know about *You*? Would You draw me near and show me what special life lessons and revelations of Your grace You want me to experience?"

As I think about the challenges or struggles where I've grown the most, the turning point was most often when my focus moved from the problem or troubling situation to asking, seeking, and being open to something the Lord wanted to reveal to me about Himself. Translation: having a fresh vision of Jesus that focuses on His character and His sufficiency—*who He is* instead of how I wanted things to change—made all the difference.

Chapter 9

I've Just Seen Jesus!

The man who has seen Jesus can never be daunted. . . .
Nothing can turn the man who has seen Him;
he endures "as seeing Him Who is invisible."
Oswald Chambers

Martha pulled the rough brown shawl around her head as she arranged fruit on a wooden tray, hauled water from the well to fill the pitchers, and did the countless tasks necessary to prepare a meal for her dearest friend, Jesus. She paused a moment to look out the window and search the road for her expected visitors. Jesus and His disciples, on their way to Jerusalem, would be stopping by their village soon. As always, Martha, her sister, Mary, and brother, Lazarus, would warmly welcome them into their home. She wanted everything to be perfect and ready for their arrival.

Jesus had different relationships with different people during His time on earth, depending on their hunger for Him and God's purposes. The multitudes heard His teachings and were desperate for the "bread" He offered; countless ones were healed by His touch and delivered from oppressing spirits. But the multitudes didn't have an intimate relationship with the Messiah like His disciples did. When they spent time with Jesus traveling and eating, He shared with them His teachings and parables. Moreover, He told them the secrets and the principles behind the stories.

But there was something extraspecial about Jesus' relationship with Martha, Mary, and Lazarus. Along with John, these were some of Jesus' favorite people, those He was closest to and loved best. That's what made it all the more puzzling why Jesus didn't come when the sisters sent an urgent message telling Him, "Lord, your dear friend is very sick" (John 11:3 NLT).

They just *knew* He would come, since He and the disciples were only two miles away in Jerusalem. Because of His powerful ability to heal and His affection for Lazarus, they had no doubt that before long they'd see Jesus walking up the dusty road to Bethany, and Lazarus would be well again.

For days Martha had labored over her brother's sickbed, wringing her hands in worry and watching at the window. *Surely Jesus got the message. Nothing could prevent Him from coming.* But their beloved Teacher didn't show up. And nothing they did seemed to help. No amount of hot chicken soup or medicinal herbs revived Lazarus.

Finally, the two sisters watched as the color drained from their brother's face and his life dissipated before their eyes, his body growing cold and stiff. Martha and Mary collapsed in a flood of tears. Added to their grief were the painful questions, "Why didn't our friend Jesus come? This would have all been different if He'd been here! It would only have taken a word, a touch, and Lazarus would have recovered. Didn't He care enough to walk the two miles from Jerusalem to help us?"

The sisters didn't have the big picture. They didn't know that when Jesus got the message, He said, "Lazarus's sickness will not end in death. No, it happened for the glory of God so that the Son of God will receive glory from this" (John 11:4 NLT).

After waiting two days, Jesus told His disciples, "Let's go back to Judea" (John 11:7 NLT). They tried to convince Him not to go because the Jews were out to kill Him, but He wasn't deterred.

"Our friend Lazarus has fallen asleep. I'm going to wake him up," Jesus announced (John 11:11 MSG).

When Jesus finally headed for Bethany, Lazarus had been dead four days. By this time, many Jews were already there, comforting Mary and Martha and mourning with them. Through the grapevine, Martha heard Jesus was coming, and she raced out to meet Him while her sister stayed at home weeping.

Martha, as usual, didn't mince words. Some might say she was bold or arrogant to approach the Savior, but I have to say a few words on this woman's behalf. Often she gets a bad rap: Martha's the driven one, after all, they say. She probably didn't take time to read the Torah. She was the sister Jesus scolded when He said, "Martha, Martha, you are anxious and troubled about many things" (Luke 10:41), and pointed to sister Mary's devotion as the most important thing. (It is, by the way!) Mary was the more spiritual sister, and her priorities were right. Not like her busy, practical sister, Martha!

But let's take another look at Martha. First, *she asked*. She didn't hesitate to send an S.O.S. message to Jesus telling Him she needed His help.

Second, she was honest. When He didn't come in time, she candidly declared, "Master, if you'd been here, my brother wouldn't have died. Even now, I know that whatever you ask God he will give you" (John 11:21–22 MSG). Martha didn't yet know that the One standing before her had the power to raise her brother from the dead. Just as most of those who walked and talked with Christ, she didn't fully understand who He was. Yet she had an irrepressible faith and confidence in her Lord. She didn't run from Him when devastated over the loss of her brother—she ran *toward Him*. In fact, she caught up with Him on the road before He even entered the village.

"I am the resurrection and the life. Anyone who believes in me will live, even after dying. Everyone who lives in me and believes in me will never die. Do you believe this, Martha?" Jesus asked (John 11:25–26 NLT).

"Yes, Lord," she answered, "I have always believed you are the Messiah, the Son of God, the one who has come into the world from God" (John 11:27 NLT). Not a bad response from one who hadn't yet seen His glory! But He must mean her brother would be raised up in the resurrection at the end of time.

Moments later, after being alerted that Jesus had arrived, Mary ran out to Him, fell at His feet, and echoed what Martha had said: "Lord, if only you had been here, my brother would not have died" (John 11:32 NLT).

"When Jesus saw her weeping and saw the other people wailing with her, a deep anger welled up within him, and he was deeply troubled. 'Where have you put him?' he asked them" (John 11:33–34 NLT). Then Jesus wept. He wasn't weeping because Lazarus was dead or because He was sad for His friends Mary and Martha. He wept because the answer was standing among them but they didn't see Him.

"Well, if he loved him so much, why didn't he do something to keep him from dying? After all, he opened the eyes of a blind man," said the naysayers in the crowd (John 11:37 MSG).

Nobody could have scripted what happened next. He who had the keys of death performed an awesome, mind-blowing miracle. When Jesus gave the order to remove the stone at the tomb entrance, Martha, ever the realist, protested, "Lord, he has been dead for four days. The smell will be terrible" (John 11:39 NLT).

Looking her in the eye, Jesus asked, "Didn't I tell you that you would see God's glory if you believe?" (John 11:40 NLT).

"Then Jesus shouted, 'Lazarus, come out!'" And Lazarus emerged from the tomb wrapped from head to toe, with a cloth over his face. "Unwrap him and let him go!" Jesus commanded (John 11:43–44 NLT).

Tears of joy flowed from Martha's and Mary's eyes when they saw their brother alive. Awe filled their hearts as they saw the majesty and glory that shone before them.

How do we know Martha was transformed by this experience? The next, and last, time Martha is mentioned in the Bible was at the supper in her home in honor of Jesus and in celebration of Lazarus's resurrection. With guests crowded around their table, sister Mary anointed the feet of Jesus with expensive perfume. Martha was still serving and was no less productive or hospitable, but her spirit had changed.

We read nothing about her being distracted over tasks or mentally anxious or bustling around. Martha's practical side didn't respond to Mary's lavish demonstration of devotion by saying, "No, Mary! We need the money for groceries!"—even though she probably contributed to purchasing the costly nard. She didn't side with Judas who said the poor needed the offering more. Her heart was in agreement with this lavish display of worship.[1] Her focus was Jesus, and the vision of His glory had forever changed her.

A Fresh Encounter with Jesus

Jesus is the Way, the Truth, and the Life, and when we encounter Him and see Him as He is, we can't help but be changed just as Martha was. Let me encourage you:

Don't sink into guilt if you are more Martha than Mary. Perhaps you've felt like a second-class Christian if you aren't like quiet, contemplative Mary who stopped everything to sit at Jesus' feet. Maybe you feel guilty if you're more like Martha, often busy and distracted doing many things. If God wired you to run a children's ministry or company and you always have so much on your plate you never get it all done, He understands. If you are a single parent and juggle multiple tasks and responsibilities, God knows how stretched your time is. Martha's serving was honorable, and as we do our work and service as unto the Lord, with our focus on Him, He receives it as worship.

You don't have to be someone you're not or try to change yourself to be more contemplative or spiritual. *It is in seeing and encountering Jesus* that transformation happens. The Lord met Martha as she was, in the midst of her life, in the middle of her grief over losing her brother, and revealed Himself to her. And just as He knew the longing in her heart, He knows the longings of your heart and will meet you there as you lay them out before Him.

As Mary did, offer all you are to Him who laid down

His life that we might experience newness of life on this earth and life forever with Him. When you turn all of your being in utter, joyful abandon, your life, though outwardly busy, will become a "living prayer"[2] and you will be increasingly aware of the Lord's presence. Give yourself again or for the first time completely to Him who created you and loves you with an everlasting love. "I despair when I try to change myself and patch myself up," said Corrie ten Boom. "I can't do it and never will be able to do it, but if I surrender myself to Him who made me, I experience miracles!"[3]

Part Four

A Fresh Encounter with Jesus through Mountaintop Experiences

Chapter 10

The Great Physician

We must realize that God's supreme purpose for granting miracles is to reveal Himself. Healing is a witness to the wonder of His Person. . . . Knowing God is the greatest miracle resulting from our prayers of intercession.

DICK EASTMAN[1]

Not again. Not this weekend, I thought as our boys raced in from their Saturday play in the backyard. Hearing our six-year-old wheezing loudly with each breath, I headed for the kitchen to get his medicine.

Asthma. When it afflicted our son, it was as if a big black cloud settled over our house. It had sent us to the emergency room when we'd driven six hours to Texas to my parents' ranch for a fun family weekend. Hospitalizations had derailed Christmas and kept our son from starting first grade with the rest of the kids. As our doctor explained it, controlling an asthma attack was like stopping a ball from rolling down a hill—you should catch it before it went very far down the slope.

Even more than usual, we wanted to head off an attack at the pass this time. My husband, Holmes, had scheduled a father-son trip to Dallas that included Six Flags Over Texas, and they were leaving the next morning. Bags were packed, and they were excited. But now this. . .

His shortness of breath and a violent round of coughing spurred me to work faster as I gathered up his inhaler, fluids, and medicines the doctor prescribed for use in an acute attack. *If all else fails,* I decided, *we'll call the doctor and head to his office or the emergency room.*

And somewhere in there I knew we'd say a prayer for him, but perhaps more as a last resort than as a first resource.

This time it was different. As Holmes and I talked about our son's condition and the special trip they'd planned, it struck us that maybe we'd been doing things backward. The doctor, prescriptions, and medical help were all important. But why not call on God *first*?

I'd read somewhere lately that God is our Great Physician, but I'd never taken it seriously or heard any teaching about it. I'd never seen God heal someone, so I was somewhat of a skeptic. However, it sounded like a great alternative to what we'd been through countless times.

So, infused with just a mustard seed of hope and belief, we knelt beside our son on the couch and asked God to give us wisdom and show us how to pray. But doubts and questions began to distract my train of thought. *Here I am asking God to heal our son, to touch his physical body and reverse this condition, but I don't really know what the Bible says about it. When does He heal, and how should we approach Him? I know that when He was on earth, Jesus healed people with just a touch or word, but does He even do that today?*

We were novice Christians, enthusiastic about our growing faith, but we'd never heard any teaching on healing from the pulpit or in a Sunday school class. Now, as my thoughts went back to the Bible, a compelling curiosity replaced the usual anxiety I felt when our son was sick. What *did* the Bible say about healing?

When I told Holmes what I was thinking, he said some of the same thoughts were running through his mind. Since by this time it was evening and bookstores were closed, we searched the house for books that might have a chapter on healing and prayer. I checked the shelves in the family room and a cabinet in the garage, where I found a study that was just what we were looking for: *What the Bible Says about Healing*. After buying it months before, I'd gotten busy and tucked it away without reading it.

Now I opened it eagerly. Our son's coughing had subsided and he'd fallen asleep temporarily, so we put our Bibles on the kitchen table, filled our coffee cups, and dove into the recommended verses, like Isaiah 53:4–5: "Surely he has borne our griefs and carried our sorrows. . . . He was pierced for our transgressions; he was crushed for our iniquities; upon him was the chastisement that brought us peace, and with his wounds we are healed"; Psalm 30:2: "O Lord my God, I cried to you for help, and you have healed me"; Jeremiah 17:14; Matthew 4:23, and others from the Old and New Testaments.

With each verse, my heart felt a surge of hope. Every thing we were reading suggested that God actually can heal people—spiritually, emotionally, and physically. In fact, I discovered in Exodus 15:26 that one of His names is "*Jehovah Rapha*, the Lord our Healer." We found specific scriptures to pray in times of sickness and began to realize that the timetable was God's, but that He invited us to cast our burdens and sicknesses upon Him and to seek Him on health issues.

Throughout that evening, we continued to work on the one-hundred-page Bible study while our two younger children ate their dinner and played beside us in the kitchen. Later, after we'd read the kids a story and tucked them in bed, we refilled our coffee cups and returned to the Bible to complete our research. There was something in the Bible, some piece of the puzzle God wanted to teach us, that we really needed. But I had no idea what it was.

About three o'clock in the morning, we read one of the last verses in the study from a passage in the book of James, chapter 5. The verse said that when someone was sick, Christians were to call the church elders to pray over him and anoint him with oil in the Lord's name. I'd never noticed that verse before. Elders praying for the sick? Anointing with oil? The church we attended didn't engage in that. I had heard the minister teach in our couples' Sunday school class that God *used* to do powerful things and that Jesus healed people in His earthly ministry, but that was then and it was over.

While the passage sounded unusual to my conventional ears, it seemed to point to this anointing as part of God's prescription. Our hearts soared when we read the next verse: "And the prayer [that is] of faith will save him who is sick, and the Lord will restore him" (James 5:15 AMP).

"Holmes, this is it," I said, my excitement building. "It's the missing piece that's never been done for him before. We need to have some elders, someone who really believes God is powerful, to come pray for him and do what these verses say."

As we thought about it, I remembered two pastors from another local church we'd visited recently. Though young, they were leaders at their church.

"Steve and Jeff! I'll bet they pray for sick people. Why don't we call them right now?" I said, feeling a sense of urgency.

"I don't know; it's the middle of the night. We'd wake them up," Holmes said.

"But doctors are on call in the middle of the night, so maybe elders are, too, if someone is sick. Because if he doesn't get better through the night, we're going to be at the emergency room with him. Let's see if I can find a phone number."

A few minutes later, I got Steve on the phone and explained the situation. He groggily but patiently listened as I told him about our son's asthma attack and what we'd just discovered in the Bible. "Would you and Jeff come and pray for our son? James says, 'Call for the elders to pray,' and you're the only ones we know who do this. . . . It's the one thing that's never been done for him, and we just know it would make a difference."

"I'll tell you what," Steve proposed. "I'll start praying now, and you all try to get a little sleep. We'll be over there in a little while."

We were so excited, we couldn't sleep. Instead, we stayed up the rest of the night, talking and waiting for the two pastors to arrive. My anticipation matched that of a child's on Christmas Eve.

At 5:30 a.m. we heard a quiet knock on the door, and there stood Jeff and Steve with guitar, Bible, and a small vial of oil. We thanked them for coming, and they went into the family room where our son was resting on the couch.

"We'd like to pray for you and ask God to make you well. Would that be okay?" Jeff asked.

"Sure."

"We're going to touch your forehead here with a little oil, just like the Bible says," Jeff explained. As the two men began to pray, nothing happened immediately. But a profound sense of peace permeated the space all around us, and we felt as if we were wrapped in a quilt of God's comfort.

As they continued praying, he relaxed and became very still. Then suddenly he called, "Mom, get a pan.

I think I'm going to throw up!" In a few minutes, the thick mucus that had been plugging his bronchial tubes came up—the very thing that happened when he was given adrenalin shots in the emergency room. Only this time it wasn't a painful round of injections causing an adrenalin rush—it was God's power.

His breathing slowed down and the wheezing gradually subsided. In a short time, he sat up and a rosy color came back into his cheeks. Steve began to play his guitar, and he led us in singing as the sun came up. God's presence filled the room and inflated our hearts with joy. I looked over at our son. His blue eyes were shining brightly and his cheeks were flushed as if he'd just come in from playing G. I. Joe in the park instead of struggling all night with an asthma attack. A grin spread over his face as he said, "Dad, I'm already packed. When are we leaving for our trip?"

As the men went out the door, our son asked me, "Did you see that, Mom? Did you see the angel standing beside me when Jeff and Steve were praying? He was very bright and shiny, all white and glowing. You must have seen it!"

We hadn't seen anything but the morning sun streaming in the windows and our son, who'd been sick but now was well. But that was enough to show us God's power and love.

Later that morning, our little guy and his dad waved to us as they drove out of the driveway in the red VW van, just as they'd planned. After they left, I dressed our two children in their Sunday best and we headed for church.

As my voice blended with all the other voices at church that morning, there was an irrepressible outpouring of thanksgiving from my heart for our wonderful, glorious Savior and Great Physician as we sang, "Blessed assurance, Jesus is mine, Oh what a foretaste of glory divine. . . . This is my story, this is my song, praising my Savior all the day long!" My joy was so full, I couldn't contain the praise, as I realized that the same Spirit that raised Jesus from the dead could actually bring life and health to our mortal bodies. That He hadn't stopped doing what He did on earth: bringing good news to the afflicted (see Isaiah 61:1). The miracle we'd witnessed was wonderful, but God's revealing Himself in the midst of us was perhaps even greater.

A Fresh Encounter with Jesus

That day I discovered that God's healing power isn't locked into the distant past of Bible times but can come through the prayers of compassionate, believing people in our time as well. I never looked at healing or at the Lord in the same way after this experience. I realized that God *welcomes us* to His throne of grace not just for the problems we have but also for our physical ailments.

I also began to discover that Jesus can heal people from crippling memories, past hurts, and emotional trauma, and that when we ask for healing, we aren't asking for something outside of who the Lord is, because part of the essence of His being is Divine Healer. Healing is part of the outflow of His love to His people.

Not only did my faith rise exponentially as a result of seeing Jesus as the Great Physician, but my husband and I began to see healing prayer as part of a normal Christian life. Jesus had a burden for the sick and hurting, and He told those who followed Him to be healers as well (see Matthew 10:7–8). God began to bring opportunities to pray for people who were sick and allowed us to witness God's healing in their lives—not because of anything about us, but because of who God is and our simple desire to be His conduits to a hurting world. The elderly man whose leg had been worse after surgery. A friend with breast cancer. A woman at church who had debilitating migraine headaches, a baby born prematurely, and on and on through the years.

I love how *The Message* renders James 5:13–15: "Are you hurting? Pray. Do you feel great? Sing. Are you sick? Call the church leaders together to pray and anoint you with oil in the name of the Master. Believing-prayer will heal you, and Jesus will put you on your feet." There comes a time when everyone needs Jesus to put them back on their feet. We can be a part of His work as we do the following:

Be willing to be a vehicle of God's healing mercy to others. "God joyfully employs an infinite variety of means to bring health and well-being to His people," said Richard Foster. "We are glad for God's friends, the doctors, who with skill and compassion help our bodies fight against disease and sickness. . . . We also celebrate the growing army of women and men and children who are learning how to bring the healing power of Christ to others for the glory of God and the good of all concerned."[2]

Who do you know who is struggling with a physical illness that you could faithfully pray for every day? Put their names on an index card in your Bible to remind you to stand in the gap for them. When you visit people at the hospital, try gently asking, "Could I pray for you right now?" instead of saying, "I'll keep you in my prayers." I've seen very few people turn that invitation down.

Study God's Word and ask His Spirit to teach you how to pray effectively for those around you who are suffering. Look up, read, and meditate on these verses: Genesis 20:17; 2 Chronicles 7:14, 20:1–37; Psalms 107:19–20, 147:3; Proverbs 3:8; Matthew 10:7–8; Luke 9:11; John 9:1–27; Acts 9:34; and James 5:13–18. Jot down beside each passage what you learn about healing from reading it. As you learn to bathe your prayers with scripture, you'll experience miracles in your life and the lives of those you pray for. And since Jesus Christ is at the right hand of the Father interceding for us day and night, when you pray for others, you are joining Him in His full-time profession, which naturally brings a fresh intimacy.

We don't know God's timetable or whether a person will gain wholeness and health on this earth or in heaven (where we will all receive new, perfect bodies), but "we can so place ourselves before the Lord, and so do the things He has bidden us do, that we will come under the influence and power of His mighty breath."[3] As you do, you will get a fresh vision of Christ as He heals the bodies, minds, and emotions of yourself and others.

Chapter 11

The Road to Emmaus

If you wish to be disappointed, look to others. If you wish to be downhearted, look to yourself. If you wish to be encouraged. . .look upon Jesus Christ.

Erich Sauer

The pair trudged down the dusty road. The seven-mile trek to Emmaus would take most of the afternoon, but the two men had so much to discuss that the time passed quickly. Oblivious to their surroundings, the men were deep in conversation about the stunning events of the past week.

"I still expect to hear His voice," Cleopas said. "I would give anything to have one more chance to talk with Him or listen to Him teach. We should have fought back! If only we'd risen up and rescued Him before it was too late. Maybe there was something we could have done." He gazed down the road, as if searching for the Master.

The other disciple nodded in agreement. "No wonder the soldiers mock us. They say the church will fade away now that Jesus is dead."

"*If* He is dead," Cleopas said. This sparked an intense conversation as they wrestled with the news presented to them just that morning. Joanna and Mary, the mother of James, and Mary Magdalene had burst into the house, talking all at once. They had just returned from the tomb, where they had discovered upon their approach that the massive stone had been rolled away. Running inside, they had found only linens. Someone had stolen Jesus' body!

Suddenly two men in shining garments had spoken to them. "Why do you look for the living among the dead?" one asked them. The women said the men were angels. But what did they know?

"Perhaps the women just had a dream," Cleopas said. He kicked a stone with his sandal.

His companion shook his head. "A dream? The women were not asleep! Why would they tell us this news unless they saw it with their own eyes? These are trustworthy women. Perhaps they *did* see the men. Maybe they were angels sent from God."

Cleopas laughed bitterly. "And perhaps the soldiers hid His body," he said. "Don't fall into the trap they set. It's exactly what they are hoping we'll do. The soldiers want to mock us and make us appear foolish! Jesus said that He would be resurrected on the third day. They realize every eye is on that tomb right now. You can be certain they will let us know where they have placed the body—once they are ready to cause us further embarrassment."

"But what if. . ." The other disciple hesitated, creasing his brow as he stared at his friend. "Cleopas, why did Jesus say that He would rise from the tomb in three days? I remember His words distinctly. Maybe there *were* angels at the tomb. It could be that we just didn't listen. Who are the foolish ones then?"

Cleopas shrugged. "Jesus is dead." He hung his head, staring at his feet as the dust swirled around his sandals. "I saw them put His body in the tomb."

They walked slowly as they continued their debate. Suddenly a stranger came alongside and joined them as they continued their journey. Cleopas stared at the man and frowned. "We must have been so deep in conversation, we didn't see you behind us," he said.

The man said to them, "What are you discussing so intently as you walk along?" (Luke 24:17 NLT). The men "just stood there, long-faced, like they had lost their best friend" (Luke 24:17 MSG).

"Are you the only visitor to Jerusalem who does not know the things that have happened there in these days?" Cleopas asked (Luke 24:18).

The man replied, "What things?" (Luke 24:19).

Both men tried to explain. It was difficult to put it into words, even more difficult to make it clear to a man who had no inkling of the wild and tragic events. The disciple threw his hands up in the air. "We must start at the beginning," he said. "Jesus the Nazarene was a man of God, and we believed in Him. He was a prophet who did miracles and taught truths we'd never heard. He was blessed by both God and all the people.

Then our high priests and leaders betrayed Him, got Him sentenced to death, and crucified Him. We had our hopes up that He was the One, the One about to deliver Israel. We thought He would throw off the oppression of the Romans and set up a great kingdom. Now all is lost. It's the third day since it happened" (see Luke 24:19–21 MSG).

Cleopas jumped into the conversation. "Some of our women have astounded us. Early this morning they were at the tomb and couldn't find His body! They came back with the story that they had seen a vision of angels who said He was alive. Some of our friends went off to the tomb to check and found it empty, just as the women said, but they didn't see Jesus and they doubt the women's story" (see Luke 24:22–24 MSG).

The stranger stopped in the middle of the road. "So thick-headed! So slow-hearted! Why can't you simply believe all that the prophets said? Don't you see that these things had to happen, that the Messiah had to suffer and only then enter into his glory?" (Luke 24:25–26 MSG).

The two men weren't sure how to respond. Maybe this was a teacher of the Law. In any case, the stranger fell into step beside them as they continued walking on the dusty road.

"Let's start with Moses," He said, as the men listened eagerly. He explained the scriptures in fresh new ways, and as they walked, He discussed the books of the prophets and pointed out references to the death and resurrection of the Messiah.

The sounds from the village reminded the men that Emmaus lay directly ahead. Children called out in play, and the smell of fish cooking over coals wafted through the air. Cleopas called out to the man when He turned as if He was leaving them. "Stay and have supper with us," he urged. "It's nearly evening; the day is done" (Luke 24:29 MSG). And He went on into Emmaus with them.

They pushed through the city streets, calling out to those who recognized them, eager to resume their discussion. When they reached the house, Cleopas started to introduce the stranger to his friends when he realized he did not even know who He was. He laughed, clapping his hands together. "We've been talking about the Messiah so much, I didn't even ask your name," he said.

The man just smiled. Then they sat at the table, and the stranger picked up the bread, blessed it, and broke it. Then He gave the bread to them, saying, "Peace be to you." As the crumbs fell to the table, Cleopas and the other disciple stared. Their eyes were suddenly opened, and they recognized Him as the light dawned in their hearts.

"Jesus?" he said. "Can it be You, my Lord?" Cleopas pushed aside his food, leaped up from the table, and danced around the room in joy as he made his way to his Messiah. The other disciple leaned over to clasp

Jesus' hand, but suddenly He was gone.

"How could we not have recognized Him?" they wondered aloud. They talked back and forth excitedly, trying to explain what had happened. "Didn't our hearts burn with fire as He conversed with us on the road and opened up the scriptures for us?" they said. "We must find Him!"

As they ran out the door to try to catch up with Jesus, the men's souls were lit as with flames. It didn't matter if the sun was setting. They didn't care if they were hungry or tired. They had seen the Savior! They had good news to share, and they didn't want to waste one more minute. Waving good-bye to their stunned friends, they hurried down the road. They had to get to Jerusalem to tell the disciples what had happened. Cleopas leaped in the air as they ran, shouting, not caring who heard him, letting all who would listen hear the good news. "He's alive!" he said, throwing his head back and laughing with joy. "Jesus is alive!"

Before long they found the eleven apostles and their friends huddled together behind locked doors in Jerusalem, cowering in fear about what the Jewish leaders might do next.

"The Lord has risen! It's really happened!" Cleopas and the other disciple shouted as they rushed into the room. And they began to tell all about their experiences on the road and how they recognized Jesus in the breaking of the bread.

A Fresh Encounter with Jesus

When Jesus met the two disciples on the road, they were long faced and defeated. They hadn't waited for Him in Galilee as the angel had instructed. Some had gone home. Most apostles hid in a room in Jerusalem behind a locked door because of their fear and despair. Cleopas and his companion had set out on the road to Emmaus. Yet Jesus showed up and walked alongside the two men. He showed up in the locked room and revealed Himself to His followers. And He is still showing up for you and me. We can freshly encounter Jesus when we realize these truths:

He's alive and in our midst. Perhaps like the two men on the dusty road to Emmaus, you know what it's like to lose heart. To feel as if everything has failed. To know your human efforts are exhausted and you're at the end of your rope. This story shows us that when we are most helpless, when our circumstances look impossible and we feel most discouraged, there is Jesus. When every door has closed in our career, when our marriage seems most lifeless or our teenager most incorrigible, Christ is in our midst. He comes alongside us in our distress just as He came alongside the downcast disciples.

And He specializes in resurrections.

Too often, however, we are unaware of Jesus' presence because we're so absorbed in our pain. Like

Cleopas and his friend, who, with faces downcast, saw only the dust on the ground and didn't notice the risen King standing beside them, we don't notice His love or blessings. We've forgotten the promises He has given us in the scriptures and can only see the dreadful circumstances. But still, in His graciousness, Jesus comes and meets us wherever we are in our pain or discouragement.

When we look to ourselves, we will continue to be downhearted and in despair. When we look to others to save us, we will ultimately be disappointed at their failure. But when we look to Jesus, our hearts will be strangely warmed and renewed just as the two men from Emmaus experienced.

We can experience Christ through communion. Just as Jesus revealed Himself in those intimate moments as He broke the bread, blessed it, and gave it to the two men in Emmaus, He invites us to draw near to Him at the communion table. We are not to partake of the grape juice and bread as an empty ritual or just to remember back to a two-thousand-year-old event. We are to receive the communion elements in expectation of the presence of Jesus in our own lives and in the body of believers with whom we fellowship. Communion is much more than revisiting a historical event. It's an opportunity for connection and intimacy with our Savior. Therefore, we are to come expectantly and reverently, with prepared hearts that forgive, worship, and praise.

As Paul said, "Examine your motives, test your heart, come to this meal in holy awe" (1 Corinthians 11:28 MSG). Ask yourself the next time you take communion, *What would I do if Christ's literal presence entered the room? How would I prepare myself to meet with Him?*

"Feed on Christ," said Phillips Brooks, "and then go and live your life, and it is Christ in you that lives your life, that helps the poor, that tells the truth, that fights the battle, and that wins the crown."[1]

Chapter 12

The Trysting Place

When we meet the Christ, the living Christ, we come to life again. With faith that springs from the depth of our joy, we run to the trash cans to retrieve the dreams and hopes we'd thrown away in our despair. Eagerly we pull them out, dust them off, and find to our joyful amazement that they are not only still intact, they are gloriously enhanced. . . . And we turn to Christ with a new light in our eyes, showing Him our dreams in a speechless thankfulness.

JIM MCGUIGGAN[1]

It's odd the way the world stops at the instant of a great loss, freeze-framing the colors, sights, and sounds around you. All these years later I still remember being in gym class and hearing the click and squawk of the public address system that foreshadowed the announcement that would forever change my innocence and that of America: *"President Kennedy has been assassinated."*

We all suffer those collective sorrows, like the moment the space shuttle broke apart. I watched the coverage, willing the astronauts to have survived the blast, willing a billowing parachute to appear. There were other moments: the Oklahoma City bombing, Princess Diana's death, the 9/11 bombings.

It was that kind of moment when Flo Perkins died.

Who was Flo Perkins? She never met a president. She wasn't an astronaut. Her death wasn't broadcast on the TV news. But in a tiny stucco house in an unknown section of Oklahoma City, Flo Perkins led a heroic life. . . .

1926. A west wind blew up dust in the streets of a small Texas town as ten-year-old Floria hurried to the restaurant where she worked. Her dark braid swayed as she stepped onto a milk crate to dry and sort the silverware. Hazel eyes shining, she watched the people who came to the restaurant to eat. The women wore elegant dresses and bright red nail polish. The men wore suits and felt hats. Children wriggled in their chairs, hardly noticing the fine food set before them.

Flor sighed, leaning against the oak breakfront that held the silverware. Closing her eyes, she tried to imagine wearing fine clothes and sitting in a restaurant to eat. With a sigh, she picked up a knife and polished it until she could see her reflection in the handle. In the dining room, a man with dark brown hair laughed at the antics of his daughter. Flor stilled. *That must be what my daddy is like.*

Truth be told, she didn't have a thimbleful of information about her father. Born in Oklahoma in 1916, Flor was four years old when her parents divorced. Since then her life had been like a line dance to a staccato beat. She and her mother moved from state to state, town to dusty town, from one restaurant to the next, with people of every size and shape weaving in and out of the picture.

After work she hurried back to the dismal rooming house where her mother rented a room, and fell into the sagging bed. Floria was exhausted. Not just from working long hours to help pay the rent and put food on the table. She was exhausted from the constant moving, never enough time to make friends before her mom shuffled her off to chase after some new rainbow. *Not that I'd have time to play with a friend if I had one*, Flo thought as she stared at the cracked ceiling.

It was longing more than labor that wearied her. Sometimes she ached with desire for something. . .*normal*. She would love to be surrounded with the same things, the same faces, and the same scenery every day. It wouldn't have to be anything fancy, no fine two-story houses or shiny new Model A motorcars.

Ten-year-old Flor hungered for the same front door to come home to every night. The same kitchen table to eat off of familiar dishes. A mom knitting by a fire and her father dozing over the newspaper. The truth was that no matter how hard she tried, she could hardly recall his face at all. On the rare occasions that she got to go to school, she labored over her penmanship in hopes that someday she could write him a letter. *Where would I send it? I don't even know where he lives*, Flo thought as she fought to keep the thin blanket around her as wind gusted through the open window.

Sundays were the worst—days when the church bells tolled and families strolled inside arm in arm. Flo had never been inside a church and had no idea why people went. She only knew that deep inside a yearning within her grew to be part of a family for whom those bells tolled.

Sleepless though exhausted, Flo let her mind travel back. . .to one little mining town in Utah where she and her mother lived for a while at the foot of snow-covered mountains. She could still smell the crisp, clean air and see the majesty of the mountains each morning. That town had been the hardest one to leave, but her heart found comfort in the stars over the desert as they drove along dusty roads in the stifling heat. She also recalled one Texas town, where she'd been assigned to an exceptional teacher who sparked a love of books and helped her learn to read.

Flo heard the creaking stairs before her mother let herself into the room. "You still awake?" her mother asked.

"Yes, ma'am."

"You might as well get up and help me pack. I heard there's work in West Texas."

Flo showed no expression as she pulled her bedraggled bag from below the bed.

In December 1928 they landed in Oklahoma City. Tall for her age, Flo looked a lot older than twelve.

"No more school for you," her mother informed her. "We need money to survive, and you've got to help earn it."

Flo lied about her age to earn a dollar a day washing dishes. Two years later, at age fourteen, she got a job at Kress, a large department store in downtown Oklahoma City. She lied about her age, and her employer thought she was eighteen. While doing inventory one day, a woman working alongside of Flo told her about the great love of her life—Jesus. Flo listened intently as she described Jesus as her Bridegroom. Flo's fertile imagination captured the image and wondered how God could come as Son and Husband.

So intrigued with Jesus, Flo borrowed a Bible to read about Him, but she couldn't understand the words. Outside her rooming house window that night she heard singing. Ever curious, she searched out the source of the sound. The music came from a small mission not far from where she lived. There was no tolling bell, and Flo had no family surrounding her, but she attended the mission alone.

The following Sunday she attended a meeting at the mission and met a young man named Oscar Perkins. Oscar walked her home and described his conversion experience. A week later he proposed.

Like everyone else, Oscar thought Flo was older. She had no idea what love was, but Oscar seemed a gentle sort and she was hungry for a family of her own. On August 17, 1930, fourteen-year-old Flo donned her

Sunday best and stood before the justice of the peace to say her vows to Oscar.

It was the second year of the Great Depression, and Oscar and Flo were dirt poor and in good company. There was no wedding cake or fancy reception. No honeymoon or shower. But to young Flo, it was the best day of her life.

Life was simple. The way she understood it, Jesus brought her a husband. Because of Him, she would never have to be alone again. A heart filled with gratitude, the same day Flo said "I do" to Oscar, she bowed her heart before the Judge of heaven and said "I do" to Jesus. In one day she became bride to two bridegrooms.

She'd learned enough at the mission to know that when she made that vow to Jesus, she was translated from the darkness of her past to the light and newness of life. She read in 2 Corinthians 5:17 that when a person comes to Christ, she becomes a new person. She lay everything—her past and her future—on the altar before Jesus and sensed a fullness she'd never known in fourteen lonely years.

Flo knew very little about Christian living but was thrilled when Oscar taught her from the Bible. They lived in a shack by the river that often flooded. But it was *their* shack, and Flo never grumbled or complained. Even though she worked long days, she rose early every morning to give praise to God.

Eventually Oscar bought a small plot of land as far

from the flood zone as he could find. There he built a tiny three-room stucco home with an outhouse. *A house of our own! I'll enter the same front door every evening! I'll put food on the same kitchen table!* Overcome with joy, Flo poured out her adoration to Jesus.

It was in that house that Oscar and Flo raised four children and later several grandchildren. It was by lamplight that Flo helped them with their homework each night as Oscar dozed. Years later they added a bathroom and an extra bedroom and converted the original kitchen into a dining room.

Every morning at 5:30, Flo knelt at the east window, which she called her "trysting place" where she met the Bridegroom of her heart. She drank in His presence and found a refuge for her soul. She found Someone who listened as she rolled the burdens of raising four children and Oscar's long battle with cancer upon Him. In Jesus she found stability and joy during every season of her life. He was her source of sanity when life seemed out of control. It was to Him that she ran when Oscar breathed his last.

So often did Flo launch her day from the trysting place that the little gray stucco house became a veritable lighthouse. Granting Flo the greatest desire of her heart—a familiar place to awaken to every morning—God allowed her to minister to generations of neighborhood children during the fifty years she grew in the home that love built.

She fed them wisdom along with cookies, crackers, and Popsicles. It was a rough neighborhood, and many of the families were as transient as hers had been. She understood the hunger of their hearts, and they recognized it. Along with sacks of groceries, blankets, and life-sustaining prayer, Flo gave to needy people she met money, Bibles, and the greatest gift of all—Jesus.

But more than anything—Flo prayed in her trysting place. She prayed for every girl and boy who lived in her neighborhood, and continued to pray for them after they moved away from the neighborhood and childhood. Young people converted in the Jesus movement of the 1970s made their way to her door and found wisdom. She taught Sunday school and taught others how to do what she did daily for sixty years—go into the presence of Jesus and talk with Him.

Flo taught me to pray. For Flo, prayer was as easy as breathing. She prayed for my children's broken bones and wounded hearts. Her prayers sustained me when my mother died. She prayed for my writing career and paved the way in the heavenlies for all the books I would write. Her little stucco home was a refuge for so many. And her trysting place was the place from which my prayer life was launched.

That's why the news of Flo Perkins's death is forever frozen in my memory alongside the deaths of presidents, astronauts, and royalty. On the cold December day of her funeral, I gathered with family and friends next to her trysting place. We sang and shared what she'd meant in our lives. I was stunned at the impact she'd had on so many lives. She had no fame or fortune on earth, but I knew beyond a doubt that all of heaven rejoiced at her homecoming.

Today Flo Perkins is reunited with both of her bridegrooms—Jesus and Oscar.

She has a home of her own for all of eternity.

Her trysting place is face-to-face.

A Fresh Encounter with Jesus

Like Flo, we all need a daily trysting with Jesus to walk God's pathway consistently through each season and challenge of life. Her life reminds me of Psalm 25:4–5: "Show me your ways, LORD, teach me your paths. Guide me in your truth and teach me, for you are God my Savior, and my hope is in you all day long" (NIV). Here are some ways to apply this to your life:

Start the day with Jesus. Naval officers used to keep their ships on course by securing a "celestial fix" on the stars. By fixing on the first stars of the evening and the last stars before daylight, they navigated and made course corrections.[2] If we aren't fixing our minds on Jesus and seeking Him daily, it's easy to drift and fall back into old ways instead of walking in newness of life.

But if we set our heart, as Flo did, on being with

our Bridegroom and having our own “celestial fix,” we can practice His presence all day long. When or where your trysting place is isn’t the main thing: what’s important is to set your heart to seek the Lord so the tyranny of the urgent won’t take away this precious time.

Be transformed. Flo Perkins experienced a dramatic transformation when she said yes to Jesus and He brought her out of a life of poverty to lasting, eternal riches. That transformation didn’t happen overnight; it occurred day after day as she walked with Him through life.

For each of us as believers, the real test of a new-found faith is transformation as well. “Faith in Jesus, real faith—accepting Him in all of His Deity, a full surrender to Him produces an incredible change—a transformation of the whole person,” says Jim Craddock, founder of Scope Ministries. “Faith without surrender is a life without living. Christians, who come face to face with the indisputable fact that Jesus does indeed have a claim upon their lives, are permanently, indelibly transformed.”[3]

Do you have an insatiable desire to know Christ and His book, the Bible? Are you being transformed as you walk and talk with Him through your daily life? Write a prayer expressing your heart’s desire to know the Lord, and if your love for Him has grown cold or been diminished from the cares and busyness of this life, ask Him to stir up your hunger and thirst to really "know Christ and experience the mighty power that raised him from the dead" (Philippians 3:10 NLT).

Part Five

A Fresh Encounter with Jesus through His Whispers

Chapter 13

The Lord, Our Reconciler

Reconciliation is not weakness or cowardice. It demands courage, nobility, generosity, sometimes heroism, an overcoming of oneself rather than of one's adversary.
Pope Paul VI[1]

As I sat on the Southwest Airlines jet about to take off from Will Rogers World Airport in Oklahoma City, I gazed out the window at Holmes and our three children waving good-bye from the gate. Tomorrow morning Mom was having a lung biopsy to determine whether she had cancer or not. We hoped with all our hearts for the latter outcome.

Only fifty-nine years old, Mom was vibrant and active and enjoyed every day at her East Texas ranch. Just a few days before, she'd finished planting her garden and pruned her beloved pear trees in the backyard. She relished spending time with her brood, traveling, and cooking for family and friends. But a persistent cough had drained her energy for months and caused respiratory infections. After trying numerous medications, the internist felt they had to do a biopsy to rule out cancer.

"Pray that whatever it is, God will heal me," Mom had asked on the phone the day before.

"Sure, Mom, we've been praying for you every day. I'll see you as soon as my plane lands at Love Field and I can get to the hospital."

Later that day, my plane soared into the air and I saw the most brilliant sunset stretched across the Oklahoma horizon. Vivid streaks of purple, red, and gold blended with a crystal blue sky and cascades of white clouds. It seemed as if God had saved the best part of His creative brushstrokes for the end of this day. I looked out the window as I asked God to give the doctors wisdom and to heal Mom. When I finished my litany of requests and sat silently, I heard the Spirit say, *"It's the sunset of your mother's life. Be there beside her. Don't be in denial."*

Naturally I want to be there for her. Mama was always there for me, I silently responded, my mind going back to all those times. Every birthday, every sickness, after school. . .Mom was there. Taking us to church, smiling from the audience at every talent show, drill team parade, and graduation. She was there to organize my wedding and help me after the birth of each of my babies. *Of course I want to be there for Mom. But by "sunset," surely You mean in the last years of her life, Lord.*

"No, she is in the sunset of her life now."

This is *not* what I'd hoped to hear after praying for Mom on the eve of surgery. I'd thought surely she could bounce back from this illness. *You could do this, Lord! Healing Mama would be no big deal for You. And she has so much more she wants to get done on earth before she goes home. Like You gave Hezekiah, couldn't You give her some more years? And please help her recover from this surgery quickly.*

"*I know you want your mother to get well, but I have a different prayer assignment for you,*" I sensed the Lord whispering. "*I want you to pray for reconciliation between your sister Martha and your mom before she goes to heaven.*"

Before she goes to heaven? I gulped. That sounded far too imminent and final. My heart sunk and tears slipped down my cheeks, for I couldn't even fathom the possibility of life without Mom. Since my father had died at age forty-seven, Mom was both mother-love and father-love to all of us. She was the matriarch of our big Heath clan, hub of the wheel of our family, the gatherer of her six children, their spouses, and twenty grandchildren for big cookouts and holidays at their Texas ranch. She was also my sister in Christ and friend.

But the instructions were clear. Somehow I was to shift my focus from praying for healing of a body to healing of a relationship.

Reconciliation. Now *that* would be a miracle. Although they loved each other, Martha and Mama had a stormy relationship as far back as I could remember. Whenever they were together, they seemed to hurt each other, and Martha couldn't get past the wreckage of the past and all the criticism she'd felt from Mom.

Lord, thank You for guiding me to pray for

reconciliation, because it must be Your plan, but this is really hard. Help me to release Mom and keep my eyes on You, trusting You to work and bring forgiveness to both of their hearts.

The next morning following surgery, we got the verdict: a virulent cancer had spread from an unknown organ and now was afflicting her lungs. Standing in the hall outside her room, the doctor told us the information like a death sentence. But the worst news was she had one to six months to live.

"Can't you do chemotherapy? Radiation? Surely there's something you can do to stop the growth of the cancer," we questioned.

"At this point, it's just not going to help. If we'd found it in the early stages, it would have been different, but it's too late. We can try some radiation treatments to slow the cancer before it spreads to the brain, but I'm not optimistic about the outcome," the doctor answered.

Too late? It's never too late for God. We rallied as a family and doubled our prayers on Mom's behalf. Her church and other churches prayed. Her pastor came to the hospital room and prayed for her many times. Scores of friends came to visit and said, "Get well soon!" adding their prayers to the mass of intercession going up to heaven on Mom's behalf. God heard her name over and over.

And every day I kept praying for reconciliation between Martha and Mom.

"Lord, fill them with forgiveness," I prayed. "Bridge the gap between them and soften their hearts. Restore their relationship and bring them into reconciliation."

I really got my hopes up when I heard Martha was coming to town to see Mama again. As I saw her coming down the hall as she headed for Mom's hospital room a few days later, I thought, *This is the day*. But when she left to go back to Houston twenty-four hours later, there was no sign of peace between these two strong-willed people I loved. My heart plummeted.

Now I confessed, "Lord, You know I'm discouraged. Give me the faith to keep praying and believing that You are able to do this."

Martha's second visit, when we all gathered for the Fourth of July at the ranch, was no better. With sisters, brother, spouses, and little cousins everywhere, they had almost no time alone to talk. By the end of the weekend, that big unseen grudge hadn't moved an inch.

And in spite of radiation treatments at Baylor Hospital, alternative treatment in another state, and megavitamins, my mother's health went rapidly, steadily downhill. By early September, only four months after the diagnosis, the doctor informed us that she had only a few weeks to live. Time was running out.

Oh, how there is so much behind the scenes that we, who see through a glass darkly, don't perceive. What I didn't know was that before Martha came back to Dallas the last time, God had been at work in her heart.

For a long time, she'd been aware of how deeply bitter she was at Mama. But she wouldn't—or couldn't—do anything about it. Martha resented Mama's "religiosity" as she called it and felt that Mama ought to finally say to her, "Okay, I failed you in this area and that area," but the apologies never came. Mama felt her second-born daughter was hardheaded, and Martha felt constantly criticized instead of supported.

At the same time, Martha had no success in staying sober. She was a serious, hopeless drunk, who was slowly and surely dying of alcoholism the same way our uncle had. She had been around Alcoholics Anonymous for several years yet had never worked all twelve steps. Lately, however, the word *forgiveness* seemed to crop up wherever she went. Like the day Martha's sponsor had listened to her fifth step: admitting to God and someone else the exact nature of her wrongs. As she finished and walked out the door, the woman spoke one word: "*Forgiveness, Martha, forgiveness*," in almost a begging tone.

So as Martha drove the several hundred miles from her home to the hospital for the last time, she went with the intent of finally finding a way to forgive. She had the desire to forgive and the knowledge that she needed to do it. But what became increasingly clear was that she didn't have *the capacity* to forgive.

"In my heart of hearts," she confided to me in the hall outside Mama's room the night she arrived, "I want to forgive her, but I can't get rid of the poison of bitterness I've carried my whole life. The more I try, the more I realize it's going to take God to do that. I don't just need a little help from God. I need God to give me the forgiveness I need for Mom."

That very night Mama went into a coma, so now the reconciliation looked even more impossible. I knew that in the weeks before, Mama had lots of talks with God, repenting for many things, even a bad attitude toward a difficult neighbor. She'd asked forgiveness and forgiven everyone He brought to mind, including her daughter Martha. But now that they couldn't even talk, how could Martha come to peace with her?

For three nights in a row, the doctor told us, "This will probably be the night she'll die. Her lungs and heart just don't have the capacity to keep on functioning." But somehow she held on. As she did, Martha's anticipation grew that somehow she'd get that forgiveness before her mother died.

On the third night's vigil, all five of us sisters were around Mom's bed. By 2:00 a.m., all of us except Martha had dozed off, exhausted from long nights at the hospital. Wide awake in the dark room, she knelt at the head of Mom's bed and held her hand. The idea came to her to let God go with her through the pages of her life, through every single thing that had bugged her about Mom, every unfair punishment, every perceived wrongdoing. She would ask God to enable her to forgive Mom for each and every one of those things because she knew surely she couldn't do that.

So as she knelt on a pillow on the cold hospital floor, holding Mama's wrist and feeling her pulse grow weaker by the moment, Martha and the Lord together marched back through those ugly times, pages and pages of the vignettes of her life. The time she was punished by not getting to go to her Sunday school picnic. Times she was spanked and felt she didn't deserve it. All the times she'd felt denied the love she longed for.

As the Spirit brought each hurtful experience onto the movie screen of her mind, she said, "Lord, forgive this for me," and then the next memory and the next. She continued on, "Let Your forgiveness flow through me for this," through her childhood and teenage years, until at the very moment when Mom's pulse ceased to beat, every hurt was forgiven. As Martha's life had passed before her, each resentment against Mom had been released. That knot in the middle of her being was gone and a sense of relief washed over her. God had done for her what she couldn't do for herself—forgive.

Just at that moment of death and release, as the rest of us slept, she saw the indescribable presence of angels around the bed tenderly attending Mama and escorting her as her soul soared heavenward. What a great gift that was.

But even greater than seeing the angels was that

with the chains of bitterness broken off, she gained the ability to see and remember all the good things in her childhood, the happy times with Mama and Papa, picnicking at White Rock Lake and ice cream outings as a family. Wonderful memories flooded her mind of Mama sitting at her pedal-driven Singer, sewing beautiful dresses for her five little daughters. She recalled her cooking big dinners and even the delicious taste of her food. She remembered how Mom had climbed out of the muck of poverty and the Great Depression from her tough Houston upbringing with her Scarlett O'Hara determination. And when the scales of unforgiveness fell from her eyes, she was also able to see the goodness and faithfulness of God for the first time in years.

The next morning when the sun came up, God's Spirit spoke to my heart: *"She has fought a good fight, she has finished the race. . .and now the prize awaits her—the crown of righteousness that the Lord, the righteous Judge, will give her on that great day of his return"* (see 2 Timothy 4:7–8).

Mama was *home.* I would miss her always, but in the midst of my sorrow, knowing that she was now in heaven seeing Jesus face-to-face like she'd told me she would and knowing my sister was free from bitterness brought a great deal of comfort.

Forgiveness began to reshape my sister's life in the years ahead and became the doorway to her recovery from alcoholism. With the exception of one misstep a year later, she has stayed sober one day at a time, by the grace of God, for twenty years. In the process, she has held out her hand to a phenomenal number of women bound by their own addiction to alcohol, their own bitterness and pain. As she shares her experience of God's power and forgiveness again and again, she has helped them walk not only through the twelve steps to freedom, but into the arms of Jesus.

A Fresh Encounter with Jesus

As I heard my sister share how God had brought forgiveness on the night of our mother's death, I saw Jesus in a whole new way as the Reconciler. I wanted Him to heal the outside, but He knew the greater needs of the heart. Mom received the ultimate healing in heaven, and Martha received a profound healing in her soul. She had other struggles but no longer was ensnared by unforgiveness and bitterness.

I saw a glimpse of how deeply the Lord cares about our relationships in our families on this earth. How the forgiveness of sin accomplished by Jesus on the cross not only is meant to reconcile us to the Father but to reconcile us to one another. "He himself is our peace" (Ephesians 2:14), scripture says, and He breaks down the barrier of the dividing wall, the wall of hostility that stands between us in our most difficult relationships. His forgiveness provides a way to restore the days that the locusts have eaten through all the misunderstandings, failures, and hurtful things we humans do to one another. He came to turn sons' hearts to their fathers and to turn daughters' hearts to their mothers, to set captives free from bitterness and resentment so they can be free to love as He loves us. Here's how we can join Him in His mission:

Be a reconciler. The word *reconciliation* means to restore to harmony, communion, or friendship. Jesus has given us, as God's children, the ministry of reconciliation (see 2 Corinthians 5:18), and the major way we can be a part of His process is to pray, laying down the tracks so God's power can come into every relationship. Is there someone you know who has a broken relationship? Someone who needs freedom from unforgiveness or bitterness? Ask God to speak to you of how He wants you to pray, and to direct your thoughts toward whatever is causing the conflict.

Get alone with God for the purpose of going through the pages of *your* life story. As you spend some time alone with the Lord, reflect on hurtful experiences and those people that caused them. Commit them one by one to Him and ask Him to heal those things that are beyond your ability to fix. As you do, you can call on the Lord our Reconciler to bring you into forgiveness and restore relationships that are broken. Perhaps, like Martha, you have seethed with resentment because you were wronged. Maybe your mother or another person hurt you or neglected to meet your needs. Hanging on to unforgiveness will rob you of peace, joy, and most of all, freedom. But forgiveness can transform your life as it did my sister's. The root word of *forgiveness* is the Greek word for *grace*, and grace is what Christ offers when we turn to Him and make the choice to forgive—grace blended with love, grace that brings cleansing and wholeness to our lives.

Chapter 14

The Power of His Word

When Jesus Christ utters a word, He opens His mouth so wide that it embraces all heaven and earth, even though that word be but in a whisper.
MARTIN LUTHER[1]

Mary passed the entrances of the market stalls that clamored for her coins. The smells of the busy metropolis Magdala once tantalized her but now nauseated her. She pushed harder, hoping to make it home before. . .

No! She wouldn't dwell on that. If she concentrated on the tasks of her day, perhaps the enemies of her mind might give her respite. Yet only yesterday she found herself in the darkness once again. Mary closed her eyes as she tried to erase the memory of the horrified looks of the innocent bystanders who stared down upon her. She pressed harder, trying to make it home before. . .

Home! Mary quickened the pace as the familiar doorway beckoned. She nearly ran through the door but paused in the shadowy sanctuary. She had ordered the servants long ago to block out unwanted light. She nearly tripped over the young servant girl who stood in the entrance. The girl anxiously looked upon Mary's face and broke into a smile when she saw her mistress's eyes.

Sanity, Mary thought, grimacing. *That's what she hoped to see in my face. Even my own servants don't know whom they will encounter from day to day.* She knew she vacillated between severe lows and highs, spells when she was gripped with panic or despair, but she had no way to stop the terrible torment afflicting her soul. Mary handed her purchases to the young girl and then slipped into her bedchamber. She laid down and pulled the luxurious covering over her entire body. *Maybe if I sleep, I will be spared.* Tears ran down her cheeks and soaked her bedding. The unwanted voices seeped into her thoughts, and she curled into a tight ball, defenseless against the angst that washed over her like crashing waves.

"What is happening to me?" Mary whispered, then spiraled down into blackness and fear. She felt hands clawing at her and shrieked in terror. She tried to push away, but something soft and suffocating strangled her as she writhed. *Help me*, she screamed silently, mouthing the words.

"Mary! Mary! Please, it's me." The tender voice penetrated her dark world, and Mary arched one way and then the other, thrashing about and reaching with everything within her to find that safe place she desperately needed. "Mary, you're tangled in your bedcovers. Please stop fighting me. Let me help you," the voice said.

Mary gazed into the face of her longtime friend

Lydia. She perched on the edge of the bed and clasped Mary's hands against her cheek. The servant girl stood behind her and trembled.

"Come out of bed," Lydia said. "Your headdress is a mess, and you've scratched yourself. Girl, please help me," she ordered. The servant took one arm and Lydia the other as they helped Mary out of bed and seated her in a chair. The servant removed Mary's headdress, picked up a brush, and began to run it through Mary's long, disheveled hair. Deeply saddened by the sight of the glazed-over eyes and sunken cheeks of her once-attractive friend, Lydia poured water on a clean cloth and bathed the scratches that ran down Mary's face. "You have hurt yourself," she said. "Were you having a nightmare?" she asked.

"You know it was not a nightmare," Mary said. She wrenched away the cloth and threw it to the floor. "I am out of my mind," she said, cupping her face in her hands and hiding her face in shame. "I don't know what to do. I can't go on living like this."

"She hasn't eaten in days," the servant girl said. Her voice quaked with fear. "I bring food to her and she leaves it by the side of the bed uneaten. We don't know what to do. That's why I called for you."

Mary looked up in surprise at the young girl's bravery, and she saw adoration in her eyes.

"I am glad you sent for me. We must get Mary to a physician. She is ill," Lydia said.

Mary pushed her friend away gently. “No, Lydia. It’s more than that. Something has possessed my mind. There are times I feel as if something—or someone—is tormenting me, trying to destroy me.” Mary grabbed at Lydia’s sleeve. “I cannot go on like this,” she said. “I don’t know where to turn.”

Lydia sat in silence, staring at her friend. Mary knew that she was shocked at her appearance. She could no longer bear to look upon her image because the hollow-eyed, stark woman she had become was so different from who she used to be. She saw the helplessness in her friend’s eyes.

“May I make a suggestion?” the servant girl asked. “I’ve heard of a teacher who is also a healer.” She smiled, and the young girl suddenly looked beautiful. “He has healed many,” she continued. “His teachings are profound and His miracles even greater. He has stirred up the religious men in the community who do not know what to do with Him—or with the crowds who follow Him as He teaches. He ministers to both the rich and the poor. He heals the sick and the lame.” She paused. “The good news is, I’ve heard that He is in Capernaum, only three miles from here. We could be there within the hour if we left right now.”

Lydia scoffed. “A religious teacher? My friend needs a doctor, not some traveling holy man. Please. I appreciate what you have done for Mary, but you are overstepping your bounds.”

The servant girl whispered, "Just the other day Jesus healed a woman who suffered like my mistress does. Her name is Joanna."

"Joanna, the wife of Cuza?" Mary asked. She had heard the rumors. They said she was mad. Something sparked in Mary's soul. She wrapped her headdress around her face to hide the deep scratches in her flesh. "Let's go now," she said and rushed from the room.

Mary, Lydia, and her servant approached Capernaum. They traveled along the coast of Galilee, and Mary stopped everyone she encountered to ask if they knew where to find the Teacher. Lydia had begged her to turn around and return home but wouldn't leave the side of her friend. Suddenly Mary stopped and shaded her eyes, looking into the distance. A crowd had gathered at the shore. "There!" she said. "I think it is the Teacher. I must go to Him." She grabbed Lydia's hand and broke into a run.

A man stood on the deck of a small fishing boat. Twelve men stood around Him as He taught. "I'm sorry," the man said. "I must go, but I will come back tomorrow." He smiled at the crowd on the shore, and they broke into cheers. Not far away, three Pharisee men stood, their frowns of disapproval lost on the rowdy crowd.

"Wait," Mary cried. She pushed through the men and women, trying to get to the Teacher. Lydia grabbed at Mary's robe, but Mary pushed her friend's hand away and rushed forward. "Please wait for me," she said.

Surrounded by His followers, the Teacher turned and looked into her soul. Mary staggered as the darkness tried to push her to the ground. Panic gripped her heart. She had to leave now. Why had she been so foolish to think that a simple teacher could help her? She turned and stumbled as people parted.

Her servant ran to her side and locked her arm around her waist. "I will help you find your way to the Teacher," she said. "Please don't give up." The girl waved her arm in the air. "Jesus, my mistress needs a miracle!" Mary staggered under the weight of insanity that threatened to envelope her. Then she heard the voice.

The Teacher's robe was wet where He had plunged into the shallow depths of the seashore. "Leave her," He said quietly. "You have no authority."

Mary closed her eyes, sinking into the darkness. "Leave her! Go back to your native hell, you foul spirits from the pit!" the Teacher said again as He touched her. Seven times she felt the piercing light as the power of His words rebuked the tormenting demons. Then peace washed over her body and mind, much like the lapping water that etched the sand below her feet.

Mary opened her eyes, and the golden light of the sun revealed the Master smiling at her. "You are healed, my sister," He said. Sanity returned to her, and a rosy tint returned to her cheeks as she was made whole.[2] Mary fell to her knees in the sand and wept with joy.

♦

Now it was months later. Mary's home was open, and light bathed each room. In the weeks after her miraculous encounter with Jesus, she had sat at His feet. She discovered that the Teacher was the long-awaited Messiah, and she gladly followed Him from town to town. She and other women of means, like Joanna and Susanna, shared their money and spent their time ministering to Him and His disciples. The hostility to Jesus had risen, and eventually the religious leaders arrested her dear friend.

She had watched in Pilate's Hall as the ruthless Pharisees demanded the blood of the Savior who was so precious to her. She listened, heartsick, as Pilate read the death sentence. She wept bitterly as Jesus was dragged from the hall, spit upon, and abused by the crowd.[3]

And now she knelt at a rugged cross. "Jesus," she whispered, too broken to gaze at the Messiah. His blood dripped at her feet. Most of the disciples had abandoned Him, fleeing into the night to save themselves, and the Roman soldiers stood nearby, their swords at the ready to kill any who attempted to help Jesus. Mary knew that her allegiance to the Master could cost her everything—her reputation, her very life—but she didn't care.

In her darkest hour, Jesus had given her life. Therefore, in His darkest hour, she would remain at the foot of the cruel cross, no matter what the cost.

"I love You, Jesus," she whispered, her heart torn with love for the One who had set her free.

On the third day after Jesus' death, Mary Magdalene was the first to arrive at the tomb in the garden where Jesus' body was laid after she, Joseph, and Nicodemus had prepared it for burial. As the first light of dawn broke through, she cautiously looked inside the opened tomb. Two white-robed angels were sitting where Jesus' body had been laid.

"Woman, why do you weep?" the angels asked Mary.

Trembling, she replied, "They took my Master, and I don't know where they put Him." Then she turned and saw Jesus standing there, but she didn't recognize Him.

Jesus spoke to her, "Woman, why do you weep? Who are you looking for?"

Thinking He was just the gardener, she said, "Mister, if you took Him, tell me where you put Him so I can take Him away and care for Him."

"Mary," Jesus said.

The familiar gentle tone of His voice gripped her heart, and she turned to Him and said in Hebrew, "*Rabboni!*" meaning "Teacher!"

"Don't cling to Me, for I haven't yet ascended to the Father. Go to My brothers and tell them, 'I ascend to My Father and your Father, My God and your God.'"

Mary Magdalene ran from the tomb, telling the news to every disciple she saw: "I have seen the Lord! I have seen the Lord!" and she shared everything He had said to her.[4]

A Fresh Encounter with Jesus

Many people in our world today, like Mary Magdalene, are tormented—and demons or no demons, Jesus can change their lives forever. We can't tell the depressed or desperate person to just "get a grip," "buck up; things will get better," or "improve your attitude and choose happiness" any more than Mary's servant and friend could tell her to snap out of her dark spells of insanity and expect her to do it.

Mary was powerless over the tormenting spirits that afflicted her, and she needed a savior and deliverer whose power was greater than the enemy. The Bible doesn't tell us whether Mary genetically inherited mental illness, a dramatic event had triggered it, or she suffered with a chemical imbalance, but we do know that with a few words from Jesus, Mary was set free forever to love and serve the Messiah. Mary's healing didn't come from self-analysis; it came from an encounter with the living Lord. And He is just as available and powerful to defeat the powers of darkness in our lives today if we simply come to Him and submit ourselves to His authority.

When you are depressed or oppressed, allow Jesus' words to nourish and heal your soul. Invite His Spirit to help you in your weakness and show you what to pray for since the Spirit Himself intercedes for you with groanings that words can't express (see Romans 8:26). Don't wait until you feel like it to get help from others—move toward other believers for worship, fellowship, and help in your time of need. At the same time, don't overlook the value of medical attention and/or psychological counseling besides spiritual solutions. God uses people in different caring professions as well as in the church to bring relief and healing.

Spend time with Jesus. "Mary Magdalene had the priceless privilege of being a member of Jesus' traveling team," says Vickey Banks in *Sharing His Secrets.* Mary didn't just have a one-time power encounter with Christ, receive deliverance and healing, and then run into the sunset to pursue her own happiness. She was willing to lose her life for Him who had given her life. And she gave Jesus "her time, her money, and her unwavering devotion. And it all happened during their day-to-day travels together."

Likewise, it takes time to develop a close relationship with Jesus, to really know Him and not just know about Him. To silence other voices and noises that clamor for our attention and learn to hear His voice so that it becomes familiar to us instead of just hearing what other people say about Him. So often we pray and make some fervent requests and then run out to take care of our to-do list for the day instead of waiting on God. But, as Banks says, "It takes time. Intimacy with God happens as the result of daily deciding to walk and talk with Him."[5] I have found our time and our devotion is *always* worth it, as scripture affirms:

> *"Whoever wants to save their life will lose it,*
> *but whoever loses their life for me will find it."*
> (Matthew 16:25 NIV)

> *The humble will see their God at work and be glad.*
> *Let all who seek God's help be encouraged.*
> *For the LORD hears the cries of the needy;*
> *he does not despise his imprisoned people.*
> (Psalm 69:32–33 NLT)

Chapter 15

The Miracle of His Presence

God's end is the process—that I see Him walking on the waves, no shore in sight, no success, no goal, just the absolute certainty that it is all right because I see Him walking on the sea. It is the process, not the end, which is glorifying to God.

Oswald Chambers

"Tonight a big group of Dutch young people are being put on a train and sent away," Corrie ten Boom heard someone say in the soup line.

"Maybe they are going to be sent to a factory, another concentration camp, or perhaps their death," another woman whispered.

As Corrie prayed for the boys and girls, God showed her what to do.

That night she crawled out the window of the washroom and hid in the shadows where she thought the prisoners would pass. It was silent except for the sound of a guard's boots crunching on gravel as he got closer. She heard low moans from the barracks as the searchlight from the tower house swept across the prison grounds. Knowing she would be beaten senseless or killed if she was discovered by the guards, she didn't turn back. She knelt in the dark and asked God to give her an individual word for each person being transported.

Then as each person walked by her, Corrie whispered a personal message just for them to each of the 250 young people who passed by her in the dark:

"Jesus is Victor."

"Fear not, only believe."

"Underneath are the everlasting arms."

After the war, one of those young people told her that all but one of the 250 who were transported that night survived[1] and how God had powerfully used Corrie's words to bring them peace not only that night but in the trials, bombing, and dangers they later faced.

This lifestyle of talking and listening to Jesus was a vital part of what prepared Corrie for the suffering she faced in Ravensbruck, called the "Concentration Camp of No Return" when she and her older sister, Betsie, were imprisoned there by the Nazis for hiding and aiding Jews.

In prison, prayer was her lifeline, and time after time, hearing the voice of her Lord literally brought life to Corrie, her sister, Betsie, and many other women. One of the first came when they arrived at Ravensbruck concentration camp. Prisoners were stripped of every possession and had to walk naked into the showers before having prison clothes issued to them. Surrendering her clothes was hard enough, but she knew she couldn't live without her Bible.

Asking the Lord to give her courage, He gave her the idea to wrap her small Bible in her woolen underwear and hide it in a bug-infested corner of the shower room. After showering, she stuck the Bible and underwear beneath her prison dress. A few moments later, she passed by the inspection station but wasn't stopped. Every single prisoner in front of and behind her was searched, including her sister, but Corrie went by untouched and her Bible undiscovered by the guards.

Daily the women were faced with suffering, torment, and cruelty. But that little Bible brought life to hundreds in the barracks of Ravensbruck as Corrie and Betsie twice daily read God's Word aloud. Corrie was already in her fifties and Betsie was several years older when they entered the concentration camp, and they endured atrocities as did all those at Ravensbruck. They stood outside in freezing cold before daybreak for roll call every day without coat or covering. They did backbreaking work and had nothing of their own—but the beloved Bible. Yet as they taught the women and encouraged them through Bible studies and church services, many came into a personal relationship with Christ. Even though they lived close to death, the river of life flowed through them.

"They were services like no others. . .in Barracks 28," Corrie wrote in *The Hiding Place*. Because of rampant fleas, guards wouldn't go in the barracks.

A single meeting night might include a recital of

the Magnificat in Latin by a group of Roman Catholics, a whispered hymn by some Lutherans, and a sotto voce chant by Eastern Orthodox women. With each moment the crowd around us would swell, packing the nearby platforms, hanging over the edges, until the high structures groaned and swayed.

At last either Betsie or I would open the Bible. Because only the Hollanders could understand the Dutch text, we translated aloud in German. And then we would hear the life-giving words passed back along the aisles in French, Polish, Russian, Czech, back into Dutch. They were little previews of heaven, these evenings beneath the light bulb. . . . And I would know again that in darkness God's truth shines most clear.[2]

As time went on, Betsie grew weaker and became critically ill. One morning she and Corrie walked around the prison grounds to pray at 4:30 a.m. as they often did before registration. The stench of death stung their nostrils. Darkness and despair hung like a shroud over the camp. Both were weakened by malnutrition and disease, and they were not exempt from discouragement. *How will I go on without my sister and the wisdom she shares with me?* Corrie thought as she wrapped her arms around Betsie. *What about Betsie's dreams of making a house in Holland where people could rebuild their lives after being in concentration camps, and her vision of our traveling around the world to tell people what God taught us in prison? Will we ever get out of this horror and back to Holland?*

As they walked in the cold, they felt the presence of Jesus as if He were there and speaking aloud. Betsie would say something, then Corrie would say something, and then the Lord would say something—and both sisters heard what He said. It was an unexplainable but wonderful miracle.[3]

Hearing the Lord speak in this way gave Corrie a whole new vision of Jesus that lifted her gaze above the suffering and horrors of Ravensbruck to the glory of heaven and our eternal hope: "We saw then that even though everything was terrible, we could rely on the fact that God did not have any problems, only plans. There is never panic in heaven! You can only hold on to that reality through faith because it seemed then, and often seems now, as if the devil is the victor. But God is faithful, and His plans never fail! He knows the future. He knows the way."[4]

Nothing had changed in their circumstances. Everything was still so terrible that Corrie thought it couldn't get any worse. They were still prisoners of people trained in cruelty and saw no outward sign of hope in that desperate place. Yet they experienced a profound peace as Jesus spoke to them. Quietly singing hymns of praise, they returned to the barracks to strengthen and comfort the women with the comfort they'd received.

Soon Betsy's legs became paralyzed and her body so weak Corrie had to take her to the infirmary. After only two days there, she died and her body was dumped together with hundreds of other corpses.

In an amazing turn of events, only a few days after Betsie's death, on New Year's Day 1945, Corrie was released from Ravensbruck. She found out later that God had used an error in the prison paperwork to free her, and at the end of the very week she was released, an order was given to kill all women her age and older.[5]

Corrie was weak, dirty, and hungry, yet on the train back to Holland after her release, she vowed to God that "she would take the message of His love wherever He wanted her to go."[6] She was elderly and her health was broken by the ravages of the concentration camp, but her spirit was strong, and she gave herself anew to Jesus to go wherever He directed and to do whatever He desired.

For more than thirty years after World War II, Corrie was a "tramp for the Lord" in more than sixty countries on every continent. She listened for God's marching orders, and then, whether her orders were to go to Africa, South America, or Asia, she went and spoke to people in churches, prisons, hospitals, and colleges. She believed with all her heart Jeremiah 33:3, which she called "God's private telephone number," which says, "'Call to Me, and I will answer you, and show you great and mighty things, which you do not know'" (NKJV). God spoke. Corrie listened. As a result, millions heard the message of God's love and forgiveness through meetings, a major movie, her books, and broadcasts on television and radio.

A Fresh Encounter with Jesus

Seeing Jesus is vital for the Christian, Corrie ten Boom believed, because "we are not ready for the battle until we have seen the Lord, for Jesus is the answer to all problems."[7] She had looked in the face of death in the Nazi concentration camp. She had seen the enemy up close.

> *I saw myself and I saw the devil, and the devil was much stronger than I. But I saw Jesus too, and Jesus was much stronger than the evil one. Because I was on Jesus' side, I was more than a conqueror! We must never forget that Jesus is always conqueror, and that we just need to be in the right relationship with Him; then His victorious life flows through us and touches others. We can never expect too much of the Lord. Hallelujah, what a Savior!*[8]

What situation are you in the midst of that makes it difficult for you to be an overcomer? Are you in right relationship with Him so His victorious life can flow through you and touch others?

Gain God's perspective. More than anything else, Corrie ten Boom's life reminds us how vital it is to see things from God's perspective. If we look from underneath the problems and tragedies, we will sink in despair. But if we look to the Lord and gain His perspective, it will make all the difference.[9] She didn't say that glibly, for she *had* been through difficulties greater than any of us can imagine. Yet none of the trials touched the clear vision she had of God's complete faithfulness, His mercy, and especially of Him as her hiding place in the best and worst of times. How do we maintain this kind of focus when everything seems out of control? By hiding the words of scripture in our hearts as Corrie did, such as 2 Corinthians 4:17–18, which says, "For our present troubles are small and won't last very long. Yet they produce for us a glory that vastly outweighs them and will last forever! So we don't look at the troubles we can see now; rather, we fix our gaze on things that cannot be seen. For the things we see now will soon be gone, but the things we cannot see will last forever" (NLT).

Ask the Lord for a word from the Bible, both for yourself and to give encouragement to other people. Maybe you feel like it's always others who say, "God spoke to me" or "God revealed this great idea to me." Jesus said His sheep would hear His voice, whether His sheep is a Dutch woman in a concentration camp or you or me. What a wonderful invitation we have! The Lord of the heavens and the earth wants to speak to us and direct our lives. And He *will* give you a word of encouragement for your friend, child, or somebody you meet on the street as you seek Him.

How do we hear God's voice amid the noisy environment of earth? F. B. Meyer suggested, "Be still each day for a short time, sitting before God in meditation, and ask the Holy Spirit to reveal to you the truth of Christ's indwelling. Ask God to be pleased to make known to you what is the riches of the glory of this mystery (see Colossians 1:27)."[10] If we carve out a little time for stillness as a part of our lifestyle, then when a situation arises where we really need to hear from God, we'll be tuned in to Him.

God is on the edge of His chair waiting to reveal Himself to you. All of heaven is waiting expectantly for you to ask for a fresh vision of Jesus that will change your life. All you have to do is wake up in the morning and say, "Today I want to see You more clearly. I want to know You more."

If we ask for a fresh encounter each day, God will reveal Himself in the ordinary things of life—through His Word and people we meet who point us to Him, through His whispers and creation, through a supernatural dream and the humblest of service, through mountaintop experiences and the deepest of valleys and trials. In fact, it's often in the extremity of our need and the muck and mire of life that we can see God the best. In the darkest places, His light shines the brightest. And He is no respecter of persons—what He did for all the people in this book, He'll do for you.

Notes

Introduction: Seeing Jesus

1. Anne Graham Lotz, quoted in *One Holy Passion*, comp. Judith Couchman (Colorado Springs: WaterBrook, 1998), 75–76.

2. Oswald Chambers, *My Utmost for His Highest* (Westwood, NJ: Dodd, Mead & Company Inc., 1935), 100.

Chapter 1. The Living Word

1. Edith Schaeffer, "God's Definition of Faith," quoted in *One Holy Passion*, comp. Judith Couchman (Colorado Springs: WaterBrook, 1998), 154.

2. Madame Guyon, quoted in Richard J. Foster and James Bryan Smith, *Devotional Classics* (San Francisco: HarperSanFrancisco, 1993), 321–23.

Chapter 2. The Psalms Prescription

1. John Spencer, quoted in Edythe Draper, *Draper's Book of Quotations for the Christian World* (Wheaton: Tyndale, 1992), #347.

Chapter 3. A Vision That Endures

1. A. B. Simpson, quoted in Edythe Draper, *Draper's Book of Quotations for the Christian World* (Wheaton: Tyndale, 1992), #6465.

2. Letter of Hannah Whitall Smith to Priscilla Mounsey, January 1, 1882, quoted in Marie Henry, *Hannah Whitall Smith* (Minneapolis: Bethany House, 1984), 104.

3. Hannah Whitall Smith, *The Unselfishness of God* (Princeton, NJ: Littlebrook, 1987), 21.

4. Ibid., 23.

5. Ibid., 131.

6. Hannah Whitall Smith, quoted in Henry, *Hannah Whitall Smith*, 30.

7. Smith, *Unselfishness of God*, 11.

8. Ibid., 141.

9. Ibid., 151.

10. Ibid., 152.

11. Ibid., 151.

12. Ibid., 153.

13. Henry, *Hannah Whitall Smith*, 34.

14. Smith, *Unselfishness of God*, 137.

15. Ibid., 163, 170.

16. Hannah Whitall Smith, *God Is Enough* (New York: Ballantine/Epiphany Books, 1992), 26.

17. Henry, *Hannah Whitall Smith*, 43.

18. Ibid., 34

19. Ibid., 46.

20. Smith, *Unselfishness of God*, 164–65.

21. Hannah Whitall Smith, *The Christian's Secret of a Happy Life* (Westwood, NJ: Fleming H. Revell Co., 1952), 236.

22. Ibid., 239.
23. Ibid., 243.
24. Smith, *God Is Enough*, 274.
25. Ibid., 247.

Chapter 5. The Face of Jesus

1. Billy Graham, quoted in *The New Encyclopedia of Christian Quotations*, comp. Mark Water (Grand Rapids: Baker, 2000), 939.

2. Mother Teresa, *Total Surrender* (Ann Arbor: Servant, 1985), 118.

3. Mother Teresa, *Works of Love, Works of Peace* (San Francisco: Ignatius, 1996), 35.

4. Mother Teresa, *In My Own Words* (Liguori, MO: Liguori, 1989), 52.

5. J. B. Phillips, *Your God Is Too Small* (New York: Macmillan, 1961), 120.

Chapter 6. An Expectant Heart

1. Henri Nouwen, quoted in *The New Encyclopedia of Christian Quotations*, comp. Mark Water (Grand Rapids: Baker, 2000), 494.

2. Herbert Lockyear, *All the Women of the Bible* (Grand Rapids: Zondervan, 1961), 30.

3. Ibid.
4. Ibid., 31.
5. Ibid., 30.
6. Ibid., 31.

CHAPTER 7. CLIMBING INTO GOD'S LAP

1. J. B. Phillips, *Your God Is Too Small* (New York: Macmillan, 1961), 88.

2. Jack Frost, "Come Home to the Father," *Charisma*, October 2002, 98–100.

3. Phillips, *Your God Is Too Small*, 33.

4. I am grateful for the works of Paula and John Sandford and their audiotape "How We See God," which brought more insight to this subject.

CHAPTER 8. THE LORD WHO SEES ME

1. Charles Spurgeon, "God's Omniscience," *Classic Sermons on the Attributes of God*, comp. Warren W. Wiersbe (Grand Rapids: Kregel, 1989), 127.

2. Spurgeon, "God's Omniscience," 127–28.

CHAPTER 9. I'VE JUST SEEN JESUS!

1. Herbert Lockyear, *All the Women of the Bible* (Grand Rapids: Zondervan, 1961), 90–91.

2. Thomas Kelly, quoted in Richard J. Foster and James Bryan Smith, *Devotional Classics* (San Francisco: HarperSanFrancisco, 1993), 208.

3. Corrie ten Boom, *Reflections of His Glory* (Grand Rapids: Zondervan, 1999), 21, 23.

CHAPTER 10. THE GREAT PHYSICIAN

1. Dick Eastman, *Love on Its Knees* (Old Tappan, NJ: Revell, Chosen, 1989), 140–41.

2. Richard Foster, *Prayer: Finding the Heart's True Home* (San Franscisco: Harper Collins, 1992), 203.
3. Author unknown.

CHAPTER 11. THE ROAD TO EMMAUS
1. Phillips Brooks, quoted in Edythe Draper, *Draper's Book of Quotations for the Christian World* (Wheaton: Tyndale, 1992), #6352.

CHAPTER 12. THE TRYSTING PLACE
1. Jim McGuiggan, *Jesus: Hero of My Soul* (West Monroe, LA: Howard, 1998), 133–34.
2. Charlie Riggs, *Practicing His Presence* (Ashville, NC: Billy Graham Evangelistic Association, 1995), 5–6.
3. Jim Craddock, *Update* (Oklahoma City: Scope Ministries), August 2003, 1.

CHAPTER 13. THE LORD, OUR RECONCILER
1. Pope Paul VI, quoted in Edythe Draper, *Draper's Book of Quotations for the Christian World* (Wheaton: Tyndale, 1992), #9438.

CHAPTER 14. THE POWER OF HIS WORD
1. Martin Luther, quoted in Edythe Draper, *Draper's Book of Quotations for the Christian World* (Wheaton: Tyndale, 1992), #6493.
2. Herbert Lockyear, *All the Women of the Bible* (Grand Rapids: Zondervan, 1961), 101.

3. Ibid., 101–2.

4. Adapted from John 20:11–18.

5. Vickey Banks, *Sharing His Secrets: Intimate Insights from the Women Who Knew Jesus* (Sisters, OR: Multnomah, 2001), 182–83.

CHAPTER 15. THE MIRACLE OF HIS PRESENCE

1. Carole C. Carlson, *Corrie ten Boom: Her Life, Her Faith* (Old Tappan, NJ: Revell, 1983), 116–21.

2. Corrie ten Boom, *The Hiding Place* (New York: Bantam, 1971), 201.

3. Corrie ten Boom, *Reflections of His Glory* (Grand Rapids: Zondervan, 1999), 92.

4. Ibid.

5. Ibid., 11.

6. Carlson, *Corrie ten Boom*, 121.

7. Ten Boom, *Reflections of His Glory*, 92.

8. Ibid., 100–101.

9. Ibid., 91–92.

10. F. B. Meyer, *The Secret of Guidance* (Chicago: Moody, 1997), 43.

Also available from goTandem

gotandemresources.com